A2 Econ

UNIT 5A

Edexcel

Unit 5A: Labour Markets

Rachel Cole

Philip Allan Updates
Market Place
Deddington
Oxfordshire
OX15 0SE

Orders
Bookpoint Ltd, 130 Milton Park, Abingdon, Oxfordshire, OX14 4SB
tel: 01235 827720
fax: 01235 400454
e-mail: uk.orders@bookpoint.co.uk
Lines are open 9.00 a.m.–5.00 p.m., Monday to Saturday, with a 24-hour
message answering service. You can also order through the Philip Allan
Updates website: www.philipallan.co.uk

© Philip Allan Updates 2004

ISBN 978-0-86003-938-9

This Guide has been written specifically to support students preparing for the
Edexcel A2 Economics Unit 5A examination. The content has been neither
approved nor endorsed by Edexcel and remains the sole responsibility of the
author.

Printed by MPG Books, Bodmin

Philip Allan Updates' policy is to use papers that are natural, renewable and
recyclable products and made from wood grown in sustainable forests. The
logging and manufacturing processes are expected to conform to the environ-
mental regulations of the country of origin.

A2 Economics

Contents

Introduction

■ ■ ■

Content Guidance

■ ■ ■

Questions and Answers

Introduction

Aims

This guide has been written to prepare students for Unit 5A of London Qualifications' Advanced Level (A2) GCE examinations in economics (formerly Edexcel). It provides an overview of the knowledge and skills required to achieve a high grade in the examination for Labour Markets. This unit's main emphasis is the issues faced in employing the human factor of production.

While this is not a synoptic paper — that is, it does not draw together the theory from across the whole A-level — there are many opportunities to use material from work in all the other units. The specification for Unit 5A contains a series of study areas beginning with the theory of competitive labour markets, followed by imperfections in the market and government policies in both the UK and the wider EU context. It concludes by looking at the practical problems that are to an extent a result of problems in the labour market, such as inequality and poverty.

In preparing for your revision programme (a process which itself should be allocated a definite amount of time), organise your notes in line with the seven major topics presented in the guide and outlined below:
(1) Labour market forces: the supply of and demand for labour. On the supply side, we look at factors affecting the size of the labour market, its age and sex distribution, before examining factors that explain the shape of the supply curve of labour. The elasticity of supply is examined — the longer the training takes, for example, the less elastic supply will be. On the demand side, we observe that the demand for labour is a derived demand — in other words, workers are only demanded because of the good or service that those workers can produce. Looking at the factors influencing the demand for labour, we start with what is called marginal revenue product. This is certainly not the only factor that determines demand, but it is a helpful theoretical starting point. The elasticity of demand for labour completes the basic theory: the more essential the skills that are required (e.g. the skill of surgery), the less elastic the demand (for surgeons) will be. So if someone has a higher skill, he or she can command a higher wage.
(2) Wage determination and differentials: the interaction of demand and supply to determine wages. Why do average earnings differ between men and women, skilled and unskilled, ethnic groups, young and old? To some extent the reasons are explained by the economics of market forces, but there is also a political and social context to consider.
(3) Labour market power: the role of trade unions and the case of monopsony. When workers club together to negotiate wages or other employment issues, there are elements of monopoly in the supply of labour. When buyers of labour become powerful, and can dictate prices and conditions, it is known as monopsony power — literally, the power of the single buyer. The government is seen as a monopsonist

buyer of health professionals, even though there is some competition from the private sector.

(4) Government intervention in labour markets in the UK and EU: governments may intervene to protect labour, but there is an implication for labour costs.

(5) Unemployment: having established that the market for labour is unlikely to be perfectly competitive, we look at another form of labour market failure.

(6) The changing structure and flexibility of the UK and EU labour markets: the consequences of an ageing population, changing participation rates and the effects of immigration.

(7) Income and wealth distribution: including the issues of poverty and inequality. Policy issues associated with these are often in the news and are therefore likely to appear on this paper. It is an area on which economists have differing views, so there is plenty of opportunity for thoughtful evaluation.

How to use this guide

This guide aims to develop A2 skills, and it should be used alongside your notes and other revision aids. The guide includes typical questions and answers, and explains what the examiners are looking for. Common mistakes are highlighted and strategies for increasing your marks are suggested.

This introduction explains the format of the paper and the skills that will be tested. It provides tips on revision planning and sitting the examination. A 4-week revision programme for Unit 5A is also included.

The Content Guidance section provides an overview of the seven main topics, identifying what has to be learnt and explaining the theoretical requirements of the unit.

The final section of the guide provides questions and answers on the economic concepts and topics in Unit 5A. There are six data-response questions covering the main topic areas, followed by A- to C-grade student answers. The answers are interspersed with examiner's comments — a helpful way of getting to know the expectations of those who will mark your papers. After reviewing the Unit 5A topics, you should have a go at these sample questions, ideally under timed conditions, and then compare your work with the answers and comments provided. This will allow you to identify areas of weakness that require further work.

Exam format

Unit 5A makes up 30% of the total marks for the A2 examination (15% of the total A-level). It is worth a maximum of 90 UMS marks (UMS stands for the uniform mark system, which scales your actual mark to one that by statistical correction makes it equivalent to any other exam). You will be asked to answer one question from a choice of two, each in four parts worth 10, 15 or 20 marks, with the marks adding up to 60.

As a rough guide to the standards required, for the June 2003 examinations the A-grade boundary on Unit 5 was set at 40/60, grade C at 32/60 and grade E at 25/60.

However, you should be aware that these grade thresholds change according to the examiners' perception of the quality of the candidates and the difficulty of the papers. In other words, these boundaries are not uniformly applicable from one year to the next.

The amount of time allowed for the examination is 1 hour and 30 minutes. You should spend 15 minutes reading through each question and sketching out a plan for each section. In this way, you will have approximately the same time in minutes per question as there are marks allocated, with a few minutes to check through your work at the end.

Assessment objectives

There are four assessment objectives, or sets of skills, in each unit of AS and A-level economics. When questions are set, these skills are very much in the mind of the examiners. The objectives are *knowledge*, *application*, *analysis* and *evaluation*. The weightings for these skills in Unit 5 are shown in the table below. It is worth noting that the weighting for evaluation is much higher at A2 than in the AS examination.

Objective	Assessment objectives	A2 weighting
1	**Knowledge and understanding:** identify the relevant economic points as outlined in specified content.	15%
2	**Application:** use the data provided and other real-world data to apply economic knowledge and critical understanding to problems and issues.	15%
3	**Analysis:** break down economic problems and issues, using economic methodology.	30%
4	**Evaluation:** weigh up economic arguments and evidence, making informed judgements and justified conclusions.	40%

Knowledge and understanding

This objective involves the ability to define key terms and to demonstrate an understanding of economic models relevant to the unit in question. In Unit 5A you are expected to be able to define terms such as 'participation rates', 'poverty', 'productivity' and 'marginal tax rates'. You are also expected to be able to show basic knowledge of recent legislation and policy changes, such as the Social Chapter (signed in 1997) and the introduction of the national minimum wage (1999). Further, you should be able to demonstrate that you understand the economic models such as the Lorenz curve as a measure of income distribution.

Application

The idea here is to show that you can apply labour market theory to the real-world case studies presented in the data-response questions. Anecdotal evidence may be used, e.g. a reference to the sex or nationality of employees at a superstore, or there may be reference to recent discussions in parliament, such as the raising of the retirement age. The exam is a data-response paper rather than an essay paper, so you will need to refer to the data in order to earn full marks in this skill area.

Analysis

This assessment objective requires some economic theory to be used, in a logical way, to break down an argument. Often the best way of answering this type of question is to draw a diagram such as demand and supply curves (e.g. when discussing wages and employment levels).

Evaluation

The key here is to demonstrate *critical distance* from the issues being discussed. All four parts of each question will require at least some evaluation, and this is indicated by command words such as 'to what extent', 'examine', 'discuss' and 'assess'. Of the marks available for Unit 5, 40% are allocated to this skill — more than on any other paper. It is because of this emphasis on evaluation that examiners are able to distinguish clearly between strong and weak scripts.

Methods for gaining evaluation marks include contrasting *short-term* with *long-run* effects, discussing the *for* and the *against* of an argument, criticising any *bias* evident in the passage, drawing out the *wider context* of the discussion, and coming to a *justified conclusion*.

Grade boundaries

Performance descriptions have been set for all A-level boards, setting the A/B boundary and the E/U boundary. These are split up into the four assessment objectives outlined above. The official descriptions are reproduced below, with the author's own examples and comments in *italics*.

Knowledge

Grade A/B boundary	Grade E/U boundary
Candidates demonstrate clear knowledge and understanding of a wide range of content, and the interconnections between different elements.	Candidates can identify elements from the specification, and some of the interconnections between different elements.

You do not need to know everything to get an A grade, but you should be able to make precise definitions of key terms such as 'participation rates' and 'inequality'.

Application

Grade A/B boundary	Grade E/U boundary
Candidates can apply the relevant toolkit (body of concepts, models, numerical and graphical techniques, theory and terminology) with clarity and incisiveness in familiar and unfamiliar scenarios.	Candidates apply some elements of the relevant economics toolkit in a range of scenarios.

You must be able to use the data, and this is a skill that comes with practice. You should remember that the questions are drawn from the data, and it is your job to make that connection clear.

Analysis

Grade A/B boundary	Grade E/U boundary
Candidates demonstrate, for the most part, ability to explain logically complex economic problems and issues with focus and relevance.	Candidates demonstrate some ability to explain complex economic problems and issues, or more familiarity with economic problems and issues that are less complex.

This skill involves being able to break down an argument in a logical way. For example, working through the classical minimum wage diagram is a basic skill, but understanding monopsony power is more complex.

Evaluation

Grade A/B boundary	Grade E/U boundary
Candidates evaluate effectively complex economic arguments and evidence, for example by: prioritisation; making reasoned judgements; presenting well-supported conclusions.	Candidates demonstrate some ability to evaluate complex economic arguments and evidence.

Examiners enjoy marking scripts that are 'clear cut' rather than 'middle-of-the-road'. The easiest way to place your script above the rest is to evaluate. Evaluation is not just having an opinion, or making an unsupported judgement. It is justifying your arguments, developing your reasoning, seeing the value of alternative viewpoints, and prioritising the options you have presented.

Even if you get parts of your answer wrong, you can still gain an A grade. Examiners apply **positive marking**, which means that what is of value will be accepted, but what is wrong will be ignored. Candidates often cross out a perfectly good piece of analysis. Leave the crossing out to the examiner — you might just earn some marks, even if it isn't the best you can say.

Planning your revision: general points

Start on the first Monday of the first clear week of the Easter vacation. Don't allow yourself to think of this as a holiday. The summer break will be much more fun if you use this one as a crammer. If you can't trust yourself to be at a desk by Monday morning, book yourself into a revision course or fix a session at the local library for free internet access. You have to be disciplined in your revision; otherwise you are wasting your time.

Educationalists agree that short, sharp bursts of revision are the most effective — after an hour or even 45 minutes your mind wanders. You must be comfortable and unstressed when you revise, although some adrenaline rush or a deadline may help you focus. Use a carrot-and-stick approach, giving yourself incentives as well as punishments. For example, going shopping — if that's your thing — should be a reward for a certain number of hours' work, or not being able to watch your favourite soap might be a suitable punishment if you haven't clocked up the hours.

Break up your revision time. Don't think that by staring at books the information will somehow magically be absorbed and that you will be able to regurgitate it. Use Post-it notes or revision cards, get friends and family to test you, write some 'night-before' notes for last-minute cramming, and use the internet — as long as you don't allow it to become a distraction.

There are plenty of interactive websites where you can test yourself as you go along. The main problem with internet revision is finding reliable and relevant material. You can waste time by looking at the wrong sites, wrong levels or wrong subject areas. There are many sites designed specifically for you. Go to the Edexcel website (**www.edexcel.org.uk**) and under 'Economics' look at pages 76–77 of the Teachers' Guide which lists the websites that you might use.

If you find yourself getting bored, stop and change tack. Examiners reward lively and well-argued responses, and anything that is learnt by rote is easily spotted. If you're bored, think how the examiner must feel!

When starting revision it is easy to get disheartened — it's easy to get bogged down in the detail, or to realise that you know very little about the UK and EU labour markets in practice and to give up. For this reason, you should survey the material for the entire unit well before you sit down to do your final revision. At this time you should:

- **Check that you have covered all elements of the specification.** The specification can be downloaded from the Edexcel website at the above address. The Teachers' Guide specifies all the areas that can be questioned.
- **Get your notes in order.** Use the specification as the 'contents' page for each section of your notes. Get a photocopy of the specification, or a printout from the exam board's website, then tick or highlight each block as you progress. Check that you have notes for each section and at least one question on each topic. If you are in any doubt about which section your notes should be filed under, ask your teacher for help.
- **Make sure that your figures are up to date.** You can get the figures from *Labour Market Trends* in your local public library. These are published every month by the Office of National Statistics. The same data are available on its website: **www.statistics.gov.uk**
- **Make sure that you cover every topic, even if you specialise in chosen areas.** The questions in Unit 5A are likely to be drawn from several of the specification topics. You must plan to cover the entire range of subjects. This will be manageable if you allocate your revision time sensibly.
- **Form a mental picture.** Under time pressure and in a hot exam hall where there is a lot of shuffling and paper turning, it is easy to find that your mind blanks out. It is useful in these moments to be able to picture a page of your notes in your mind, and work from there. This means that during preparation you need an orderly system, and you must be very clear in your layout. Recall is also easier if you revise in the same conditions as those you will experience when writing the exam paper. So switch off the music and learn to ignore the phone ringing.

- **Make use of your friends and family.** Arguments are not always a bad thing. By disputing the issues you will see both sides of a question, and by defending yourself you will develop all the skills needed for evaluation.
- **Time yourself.** Ask your teachers if you can submit some of your homework as timed pieces. But make sure that you get your notes clearly sorted before you set the clock — don't just write off the top of your head. There are practice questions in this book; you can find others on the Edexcel website and in current journals such as *Economic Review*. Many students find this the best way to gain confidence in exam preparation.
- **Be informed.** You need a daily dose of current affairs, and quality broadsheets and television/radio news often cover economic issues. Anecdotal evidence, in the form of examples from the world around you, is also helpful for application of the subject content. For example, you may notice that most refuse collectors are male and most cleaners female in your location. Ask yourself why this is. Important conclusions can be drawn from these simple observations.

A 4-week structured revision plan

Day	Week 1	Week 2	Week 3	Week 4
One	The UK and EU context of labour markets	Wage differentials	Unemployment	Ageing
Two	The demand and supply of labour	Discrimination	Government intervention: NMW	Measuring distribution of income (Lorenz)
Three	Elasticities	Trade unions	Government intervention: WTD and equal pay	Current distribution of income and wealth; poverty
Four	Wage determination	Monopsony	Government intervention: mobility and flexibility	Changing the distribution of income and wealth
Five	Exam practice: data-response question from this guide	Exam practice: data-response question from this guide	Exam practice: data-response question from this guide	Exam practice: data-response question from this guide

For final revision in the weeks leading up to the examination, you could write summaries of your notes — crammer cards or 'night-before notes' will help you to be sure of the basics from which to build your arguments in the exam. You could also add key dates and use a colour coding system. Half an hour a day for a fortnight has much greater value than a day of solid revision — and it might also be more interesting. Your mind will play with the ideas when you are not sitting at your desk, and you will realise that there are gaps in your understanding that you can address when you go back to your notes the next day.

How to answer the questions

The data-response questions for Unit 5A tend to come from newspaper and magazine articles. It is therefore well worth your while getting into the habit of reading a broadsheet newspaper such as the *Financial Times*, *Guardian*, *The Times* or *Independent*, reading BBC Online or *The Economist*, listening to Radio 4 before 9 a.m. or watching *Newsnight* at 10.30 p.m., and asking yourself whether the articles would make good Unit 5 questions. Question the journalism, don't just accept it. Give reasons why there might be bias. It is eye-opening to read about the same event in different newspapers. Try to detach yourself from the viewpoint of the journalist and offer an opposing view.

You should be up to date in your knowledge of the main trends in the economy at the time of the examination and for the previous 5 years or so. You should also have a good understanding of the UK policy framework and some knowledge of international current affairs — especially the changing nature of the EU.

In the summer 2003 paper, *all* the essay sections were evaluative, beginning with key words such as 'examine', 'assess' and 'evaluate'. It is therefore vital that you adopt a critical approach. Avoid the temptation of reeling off all you know about a subject without structuring your answer to the actual question set. Be sure to come to an evaluative conclusion at the end.

Further tips

- **Choose your question carefully.** You have 15 minutes to read through the questions and, although you might see other candidates starting in the first minute or so, you might also see them crossing through whole pages when they realise they have started the wrong question for them. It is better to be able to have a reasonable go at *all* parts of the question than to answer a question where you might be really confident on one part but have to bluff your way through another. Examiners are trained to spot waffle.
- **Think through your answer — sketch out a plan if this helps you.** For a 10-mark question you should have two points; for a 15-mark question, three points; and for a 20-mark question, four points are expected.
- **Look carefully at the demands of the question.** If you are asked to give *consequences*, don't waste your time by explaining *causes*. If you are asked for *possible* policy changes, don't give ones that have already been introduced. If you are asked for changes in *income* differentials, do not address *expenditure* directly.
- **A picture saves a thousand words.** Use diagrams to explain your answers but make sure that they are relevant. Label them correctly, or they will not add to your marks. The most common diagrams will be those plotting wage against the quantity of labour, or cumulative incomes against the population (the Lorenz curve). Shifting elements of your diagram will earn easy analysis marks, and if you can introduce the concepts of elasticity or changes over time, you are likely to earn evaluation marks. Make sure there is enough space on your diagrams to add arrows to show changes that you may want to use as part of your analysis.

- **Be strict with your time allocation for each question.** If you think of a minute to a mark, you will have a few minutes left at the end of each question. Leave a gap at the end of each answer, so that you can add further evaluation as your mind continues to process the question as you go on to the next one. Try to avoid using asterisk marks and continuations at the end of your answers. Although examiners will read these, you will lose their train of thought if your answer is disjointed.
- **Choose the question you can tackle best overall, rather than the one where one part is your favourite topic.** The problem with choosing a question where you know one part really well is that you might become complacent, or miss the point on the other questions. Candidates get very excited when they see a question that they have attempted before, but this leads to surprisingly bad performance. If the question is worded slightly differently, whole chunks of the answer might get marked as 'not relevant'.
- **Use economic terms precisely.** Define the key terms in the question, and continually return to the question to ensure that your answer is relevant.
- **Use 'signposts'.** It may be clear to *you* where your argument is going, and writing 'first', 'second', 'third' etc. might feel clumsy. But this gives your writing a structure, and makes it easier for the examiner to concentrate on content and not get lost in your style. It is also worth making it very clear to the examiner where you have attempted to gain evaluation marks. You can do this by starting a sentence or paragraph with such words and phrases as, 'however', 'on the other hand', 'in the long run' and 'it depends'.
- **Justify your conclusion.** Ideally each paragraph should contain a partial conclusion. This should be a summing up of the stage that you have reached in your argument, building up to an overall judgement of the issue that the question poses. When you start each paragraph, look again at the question and check that your answer is still relevant, and when you reach the conclusion, you could return to the wording of the question with a direct answer. However, don't be too bold — there is rarely a straight yes or no answer. Whatever your conclusion, there are always going to be problems, and these should be stated.
- **Identify the economic theory behind the question.** Questions tend to be set with economic theory in mind. If at all possible, use the relevant theory rather than writing a general answer. Don't hesitate to use theoretical diagrams and economic terms in your answers.
- **Make use of the text or data provided.** This is a data-response paper, not a set of four abstract essays. While not all the answers will be embedded in the text, you will be able to use the text or data for each part. If you do not do so, you will fail to pick up easy marks. However, don't use more than a few words in quotation marks, and remember that the data might not be accurate or unbiased. If you can comment on the possible unreliability of the data, you will earn evaluation marks.
- **Look at the scale of graphs.** There may be a scale on each side, which helps you to spot patterns, but these must be used carefully, as you identify which data relate to which scale.

- **When the mark base is higher, go deeper.** You cannot be expected to evaluate *every* relevant point, and the cost of covering every issue is that you cannot attempt to unravel the complex issues. Bullet points are signs of information being learned — assessment objective 1, but little more. You should instead write solid paragraphs which develop each point, and give examples and counter-arguments.
- **Focus.** Address the words in the question in your introduction — for example, does the question make any assumptions? This will put you on an evaluative footing from the start. Don't be content with simply defining the words in the question: try to highlight a critical issue or theme. Keep your eye on the question throughout your answer. Any irrelevant material will have a line drawn through it, earning zero marks. Think of the opportunity cost!

Content
Guidance

The Labour Markets option of Unit 5 combines both theory and applied economics relating to the human factor of production. The framework is set in a European context, not just the UK. The content of Unit 5A can be broken down into a general introduction and seven main headings:

- Introduction to labour markets: the EU context (p. 17)
- Labour market forces (p. 18)
- Wage determination and differentials (p. 21)
- Labour market power: the role of trade unions and the case of monopsony (p. 24)
- Government intervention in labour markets in the UK and EU (p. 29)
- Unemployment (p. 33)
- The changing structure and flexibility of the UK and EU labour markets (p. 37)
- Income and wealth, including the issues of poverty and inequality (p. 40)

Introduction to labour markets: the EU context

Unit 5A is an **application** of market theory to one particular factor of production — the workers. It is set within the context not just of the UK but also of the EU as a whole. Many textbooks focus on the UK, but you should not be surprised to see data in the exam based on, say, Italy's pension crisis, France's powerful unions or Germany's high wage costs. The theory is, of course, the same for whichever country is being considered, and you will not be expected to have any specific knowledge about other countries. However, it is important that you understand the importance of EU law over and above UK legislation, and the recent developments in policy that apply to all EU countries, especially since the signing of the Social Chapter in 1997.

Background from Units 1, 2, 3, 4 and 6

The **operation of markets** and their ability to allocate resources efficiently (Unit 1) is the concept used for wage determination. Price elasticity of demand and supply helps to explain why wages and employment levels differ in different markets. **Market failure** (Unit 2) is the underlying concept for explaining minimum wages and monopoly. Unit 3 is useful for considering the causes, costs and consequences of **unemployment**, the relative merits of demand- and supply-side policies, and the distinction between income and wealth. The Unit 4 model for **monopoly**, where marginal revenue is twice as steep as average revenue, is a useful diagram for explaining trade unions, and with some logical steps we can arrive at **monopsony**. It is helpful to consider the alternative motives of firms for this unit — are all firms profit maximisers? You would be rewarded for introducing **conflicts** between macro-economic policies (Unit 6) where relevant: for example, 'cutting taxes as an incentive to workers may have inflationary effects' would be a helpful observation on the Labour Markets paper, although no specific analysis from Unit 6 is required.

Aggregate and disaggregated data

All of the work you will be required to do in this unit is based on data that will be given to you. 'Aggregate' means 'clubbed together' or 'total'. **Aggregate data** give overall trends, e.g. unemployment is continuing to fall; **disaggregated data** are broken down and might tell a different story, e.g. male unemployment is rising while female unemployment has fallen to its lowest ever level. The data might be placed in order of ascendancy and then split into **deciles** (10% chunks) or **quintiles** (20% chunks). Once disaggregated it is easier to analyse changes, say, in the distribution of income. If the top and the bottom deciles are on average further apart, then the income gap is widening. It is no help to look at just the top and the bottom 1% — there may be distortions that make the data meaningless. For example, footballers' salaries are sometimes extraordinary, but footballers are so few in number that the inequality issue is not significant.

- Many people are aware of the UK's 'opt-out' of the Maastricht Treaty in 1991, but few recognise the 'opt-in' implications of signing the Social Chapter.
- The single European market (in effect since 1 January 1993) has meant that workers as well as goods and services can move freely around the EU. Within the mainland EU countries, this has vastly increased the flexibility of labour markets. For UK citizens there are still strong language and cultural barriers.

Useful exercises
- There are articles in the broadsheets every day relating to EU labour market issues, as well as in the weekly newspapers. As you read them, try to note down issues relating to the flexibility of labour markets.
- Enter a debate with some classmates about why UK firefighters earn about £5,000 more than French ones. Why don't the French firefighters move to the UK? How can the firefighters in the UK make such an impact by going on strike? What would increased German flexibility do to UK unions in the car industry? Why does BMW like to build cars in the UK? Why are Spanish firms setting up so many service agencies in the UK? Are language barriers within the EU a short- or long-run problem?

Links with other units
- The EU context is closely related to 'international competitiveness and government policies to enhance the UK's relative position' (Unit 6).
- The principles of how markets work (Unit 1) is an underlying theme, closely linked to why markets fail (Unit 2).

Labour market forces

Supply of labour

Two main factors determine the shape of the labour supply curve:
- **The substitution effect.** As wages rise, the next best thing, leisure, is costing us relatively more; the opportunity cost of work rises. The effect of this on supply is called the substitution effect — we offer work instead of taking leisure as wages rise. Substitution will always have a positive effect on the supply of labour, wages against hours worked, because as wages rise the opportunity cost of working always rises. However, the effect is unlikely to be linear. There is a time when the impact will lessen, as workers will have accumulated sufficient wealth.
- **The income effect.** The supply of labour is distinguished from the supply of non-human factors of production in that there is value to be gained by not working (leisure) as well as the reward for work (wages). Most of us would say that we would prefer not to work if we could afford it — in other words, if incomes were high enough, our supply of labour would be less. This could explain a backward-bending supply curve for labour (see the diagram below). The income elasticity of

demand for leisure is high (we respond greatly in our demand when our income changes), so this exaggerates the effect. At wages above W_m the negative income effect outweighs the positive substitution effect, and the worker offers fewer hours for higher wages.

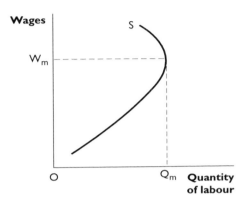

For example, suppose you ask your economics teacher for extra lessons. Maybe if it's just you, she will charge very little. But once word gets around and all your class-mates want lessons too, the price will go up to induce her to do the extra hours. There will come a point where she will only take on an extra lesson, perhaps, if the pay is really good. And if it is that good, she can afford to take a longer holiday, and you might have to start missing lessons as she takes time off to spend her holiday money. The supply curve bends backwards.

Demand for labour

The demand for labour is a **derived demand** — in other words, workers are demanded only because of the good or service that those workers can produce. The greater the value added by the worker to the final price of the good or service, the more you would expect the worker to be paid. The more price inelastic the demand for the final product, the more wages can be raised. In competitive markets, workers will be employed up to the point where they cease to add profit to the firm. At this point, a firm will either stop producing or switch to another factor of production such as machinery.

In theory, the demand for labour is based on the value that each extra worker provides in a business — the **marginal revenue product (MRP)**. It is found by first measuring the actual amount that an extra worker produces. This is multiplied by the amount that the output could be sold for. The final figure (MRP) is the most that the firm would be willing to pay for that worker. According to the law of diminishing returns, the amount that extra workers produce will eventually decrease. It is easy to assume that the extra output will be sold at either the same price or less than the product already on the market, so the overall MRP will be downward sloping.

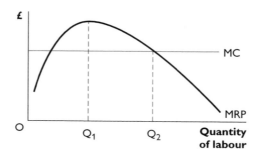

Q₁: The law of diminishing returns sets in

Q₂: Maximum profit for employer; equilibrium
point in perfectly competitive model

The maximum profit to the employer occurs where marginal profit is zero: that is, where MRP = MC. MC is the wage, often drawn horizontally on the assumption that the firm can pay any extra worker the same as existing workers (the perfect competition assumption).

For example, imagine that you own an orchard. The number of apple pickers you employ depends on the amount that the apple pickers cost, how much you can sell the apples for, as well as the amount of apples that you have. One apple picker working alone might not be very productive: although it would be easy to reach the apples, there would be no one to hold the ladder or move it or pass the full buckets to. Two is often better than one — the marginal physical product may indeed increase at first. But as you take on more apple pickers, the apples get harder to reach, and smaller and maybe less ripe ones will have to be included in order to keep everyone busy. You might find that you don't have enough buckets or ladders or other tools, so sharing goes on, which wastes time. It is certain that you will eventually reach a point where an extra worker produces less than the last. And it is likely that the more that you have to sell, the less you will have to charge. You keep on employing apple pickers until the value of their output is exactly equal to the wage the picker wants: wage (or MC) = MRP.

Examination skills and concepts

- The supply of labour is determined by a combination of income and substitution effects.
- The demand for labour is determined in competitive markets by the value that each extra worker adds to the firm.
- Wages are in equilibrium where demand equals supply. In a competitive model, this is where MC = MRP.

Common examination errors

- Some students get very confused with MRP = wage. Why doesn't the employer stop before wage is equal to the MRP? The answer is the same as with MC = MR

(Unit 4). The employer makes a profit on every worker up to the last worker, and therefore maximises profit by employing all the profitable units of labour, even when the *marginal* profit on the last worker is infinitely small.

- MRP theory is useful for explaining demand for labour, but it is not the only factor determining demand — if, indeed, it is a determinant at all in some cases. You must remember that it is the sole determinant only in the competitive model.

Links and common themes

- Marginal analysis is a useful and neat piece of economic methodology with which you will have become familiar in Unit 4.
- The backward-bending supply curve is a useful way of demonstrating the income and substitution effects, but do not feel that you have to draw all labour market supply curves in this way. They can confuse your further analysis.

Wage determination and differentials

Price theory is the basic toolkit in microeconomics: in a free market, where the economy is not run by governments, **prices are determined by the forces of demand and supply**.

If prices are too *high*, supply is greater than demand and there is an excess of the good or service. To get rid of surplus stock, firms will cut their prices. As they do so, fewer firms will be willing to compete (contraction of supply), and there will be an extension along the demand curve, as more is demanded at a lower price. The process stops where demand equals supply, and there is no longer any excess stock.

If prices are too *low*, there will be shortages. The deficit will cause queues or waiting lists, and shop shelves will be empty. Firms will realise that they can increase their prices and still sell everything. They may increase supply — perhaps increasing costs by getting their staff to work overtime — and there is an expansion along the supply curve. As prices rise, so demand contracts. Again, the process stops where demand equals supply. This point is called **equilibrium** — it's a *balance* point because there is neither surplus nor deficit and there is no tendency for the price to change.

The same explanation can be used for **wage determination**. Wages are the price of labour — put this on the vertical axis instead of price. The chief difference with this diagram compared to the normal market diagram is that **supply is by workers** and the **demand is by firms**; remember that this is a factor market (demand and supply of factors of production), not a product market (demand and supply of goods and services).

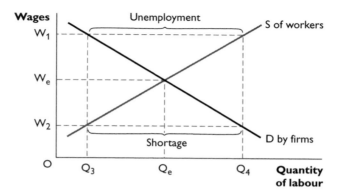

Where there are shortages of a type of labour, wages rise. If a job is unskilled, there is likely to be more labour on offer, so prices will be low. Price (or wage) theory explains why:

- Newspaper deliverers earn less than refuse collectors because refuse collection is dirty and dangerous work. The supply of workers is therefore low.
- Nurses earn less than doctors, as the skills and length of training required of doctors keeps their number down.
- Football stars command high salaries — the demand for famous players is extremely inelastic, while the supply is perfectly inelastic.
- Many professional actors earn less than bricklayers because of skill shortages in the construction industry.
- This economic theory can to some extent explain why women earn less than men on average: there is a crowding of people who want to work in jobs with more flexible hours, 'lighter' work and the possibility of working part time. Wages are effectively bid downwards in these jobs, where women are usually employed.

Wage differentials are the gaps between different wages. Explanations of these are both economic and non-economic. If one worker produces more than another and they are being paid per unit produced (piece-rates), the one producing more will obviously be rewarded for his or her higher productivity. Some people are prepared to work longer hours and if they are being paid per hour (time-rates), they may also find that they are on a higher wage owing to overtime payments. Those factors that determine wage differentials follow the same principle as the factors that determine wages for a profession as a whole, and again there are discrimination issues that also determine why differentials occur.

Discrimination occurs when wages differ for reasons that are unrelated to the value of the output of the worker, e.g. due to sex, age, ethnic origin or possibly location. Discrimination was made illegal in the 1970 Equal Pay Act and the 1976 Race Relations Act. Consequently, while much discrimination still exists, it is often covert.

Reasons why wages differ which are not solely explained by the value of economic output include the following:

- **Social, political and historic influences** have meant that women often earn less than men. In fact, the UK has the widest gender pay gap in Europe (women earn 82% of male earnings, according to the Equal Opportunities Commission, 2003).

- Women are thought by some to be subject to a **glass ceiling** when it comes to promotion. It is as if an invisible force prevents upward movement, keeping them in less responsible jobs. The reasons are partly economic: women are more likely to take time off for child rearing and may have had a career break which means their training could be uneven. But it is also argued that there is a social factor whereby men (who do most of the recruitment and offer the promotions) tend to promote men. There are some notable female managers, but the percentage of senior management positions held by women is low.
- **Lack of reliable childcare** means that women cannot return to work and take a more senior position. There are initiatives in the UK currently aimed at restoring a healthy work–life balance, including more flexible treatment of working parents of either sex. This should ensure higher long-run productivity.
- **Ethnic groups** are often paid at a lower rate, and while this may be due to lower skill there are often other factors, such as the location and geographic immobility, cultural issues or language, and perhaps pure prejudice.
- **Age** may also be a factor in wage determination, although the relationship is not straightforward. Older workers may have more skills and experience and be more reliable, whereas younger workers may be more dynamic, adaptable and geographically mobile. Apart from these economic factors there may be discrimination against certain age groups within a profession: some superstores, for example, deliberately employ older workers, whereas many stockbroking firms prefer young blood.
- There is a **geographical divide** between London and the southeast on the one hand and the rest of the UK on the other. Housing markets also have a knock-on effect on wage differentials.

The importance of elasticity in wage determination

Elasticity measures responsiveness. If wages go up, more people are willing to supply their time. How can we predict how many more worker-hours will be supplied? Similarly, when wages go up, fewer workers will be demanded, but by how much will this demand contract? This elasticity of supply and demand is in itself determined by a series of factors.

Factors determining the elasticity of demand (of firms)	Factors determining the elasticity of supply (of workers)
Elasticity of demand for the final product	Skills required
Percentage of costs accounted for by labour	Length of time needed to acquire education or training
Ease of substitution of workers for machines	Costs of education and training
Expectations of future demand	Mobility
Costs of relocation of production abroad	Quality of working environment, including benefits and flexibility

If wages change, the extent of the change along demand and supply curves depends on these factors. The less elastic the demand or supply is, the more the wage will have to change to cause a change in quantity. High-skilled jobs are often highly paid for this reason: the skills and length of training required make the elasticity of supply very low. By contrast, where demand or supply is elastic, a small change in wage will have a large impact on quantity. Low-skilled jobs are often lowly paid for this reason: a small increase in wages will attract vast numbers of workers, so employers don't have to raise wages very far.

Examination skills and concepts
- Essentially the more skills that are required, the less elastic the demand will be. Therefore, if someone has a higher skill, he or she can command a higher wage by restricting supply. This is arguably what lawyers do.
- Discrimination is one reason why equally skilled and experienced people are paid different amounts for doing the same job.

Common examination errors
- Confusion over demand and supply elasticities — the demand depends on the firm, and the supply on the worker.

Links and common themes
- Wage determination is an application of the theory of demand and supply (Unit 1), so remember the importance of elasticity to give depth to your analysis.

Labour market power

The theory so far applies to competitive markets, where there are many buyers and sellers of labour, and no one firm or worker can influence wages. It assumes that there is perfect knowledge and mobility, that all firms aim to maximise profit, and that employers and workers are rational, i.e. they make decisions by reasoning and not on the basis of emotions. In practice, perfect competition does not exist, but the model can be seen to work in some situations. For example, the demand and supply of unskilled labour such as agricultural workers is fairly elastic and the market for agricultural workers demonstrates many characteristics of competitive markets.

Monopoly and **monopsony** in labour markets are contrasting models, where the markets are not perfectly competitive. Monopoly means **single seller** and in the labour market refers to workers joining together in trade unions to sell their labour. When all workers club together in a single union, they have the power to control not just wages and employment levels, but also rights, conditions of work, holidays and so on. Monopsony means **single buyer**: we look here at the power of firms to control — even exploit — their workers. Monopsony theory is a neat mirror image of monopoly theory.

Monopoly labour supply: the role of trade unions

Collective bargaining

When trade unions are brought into the analysis of wage negotiation, the union represents workers as a group (*collective*) and has a degree of monopoly power in the negotiation of wages (*bargaining* with the employer). If the employer is large and powerful, such as the government, a strong union has traditionally been seen as necessary for the individual to have his or her voice heard. The threat of several thousand members of a public sector union walking out on strike is far more worrying to the government than one person entering into a dispute. Unions may try to exploit the monopsony profit that powerful employers might have (see p. 27).

Bargaining can be at a local or national level. **Local bargaining** occurs when there is an issue as to whether workers doing the same job in different parts of the country should be paid different wages to reflect the different costs of living: for example, the 'London weighting'. **National pay bargaining**, preferred by trade unions in general, often takes place when all workers are given the same basic salary for doing the same job. The problem with this is that some regions find it very hard to get any job applicants (for example, teachers in the Home Counties).

Recent trends in union membership

The role of trade unions has changed over the last 25 years. In the 1970s, unions were powerful in wage negotiations and there were knock-on effects from one union to another. Whole industries could come to a standstill within minutes. Steelworkers would strike, not for their own grievances, but to add support to the cause of the coal-miners; car-builders would 'walk out' if there were problems on the railways. Anyone not going along with industrial action could be bullied and labelled a 'blackleg' or 'scab'. Nowadays the unions have less influence, and it is hard to imagine unions in the UK causing the same disruption to the economy that the French unions, for example, can inflict. There are two main reasons for this: legislation and falling membership.

Legislation

The Conservative government under Margaret Thatcher (1979–90) enacted a series of measures aimed at curbing the power of the unions. Specifically, the following union activities were outlawed:

- **Secondary strikes.** These involved the practice of striking in 'sympathy' with another union so as to enlarge the impact of the original industrial dispute. Secondary action during the 1970s and early 1980s reached its height in the 'Winter of Discontent' (1978–79) and was made illegal in the Employment Act (1980). It is, however, still very common in other EU countries, such as France.
- **Unballoted strike action.** Striking was made illegal unless supported by a majority of union members who had voted at least 7 days in advance in a secret ballot (Trade Union Act 1984). The failure of the National Union of Mineworkers to conduct such a ballot in the miners' strike of 1984–85 caused deep divisions within the union and contributed to the failure to achieve the striking miners' aims.

- **Closed shop agreements.** The practice of *requiring* union membership for workers within a firm was seen as an infringement of individual liberty and detrimental to the supply of labour.

Although often characterised as being politically motivated, the aim of the Conservative government union reforms was to make the labour market more responsive to economic change, and many would argue that the UK labour market is more flexible than those of other EU members.

Falling membership

The second main factor in the changing role of trade unions is the significant decline in union membership. At their peak in 1980, union numbers were about 13 million (54.5% of the workforce); in 2003 they stand at around half that, about 6.7 million (26% of full-timers). Union membership has fallen for many reasons:

- The legislation described above has made it less worthwhile to be in a union. Along with measures to curb the power of the unions, the Thatcher government legislated to protect the individual in the workplace, a role that historically had been taken on by the unions.
- The power of unions has become much weaker in some industries due to the changing market. An example is car manufacturing, which is increasingly internationally competitive. The incentive for industrial action in this sector has diminished since, given overcapacity within the industry as a whole, employers have had the potential to move production to more efficient plants elsewhere. Strike action could well be detrimental to job security. This is particularly true of the UK where car manufacturing is almost entirely foreign-owned. The union at the Peugeot factory in Ryton near Coventry stopped short of strike action in 2003 owing to threats that production would be moved abroad.
- The decline of manufacturing industries in the UK has also had an impact on union membership. Traditionally heavily unionised, these industries have largely been replaced by the tertiary service sector in which the workforce has a different profile: there are more women and part-time workers, who often have less incentive to belong to a union. It is true that the 'wildcat' (unballoted) strike of check-in staff at Heathrow airport in July 2003 was catastrophic for British Airways in terms of marketing, but its passengers could at least be moved on to other airlines.
- Now that more workers are also 'stakeholders' in their firms — that is, they gain financially when the company does well — they are less likely to act in a way that is harmful to their employers' profits. It may be that recent declines in the stock markets will reverse this effect, as resentment builds up among workers who have received shares instead of pay.
- The fall in union numbers itself causes a fall in numbers joining. Why join when so many are leaving or not joining, and the union is seen to be becoming less powerful?

However, union membership appears to have stopped falling, and indeed there have been small increases in some sectors. A number of factors help to explain this:

- Unions still fulfil their traditional role of collective bargaining. In situations where the employer is particularly powerful (see 'Monopsony' below), or where the employer is the public sector (such as in the firefighters' strike, 2002–03), union membership greatly enhances the position of the individual employee in wage negotiations.

- Since the 1990s, unions have diversified and to some extent rebranded their image. In place of the militant unionism of the 1970s and 1980s, union leaders often adopt a more conciliatory approach to industrial disputes. In addition, unions provide legal advice and protection for individual members — a role that has particular relevance to white-collar workers such as teachers.
- Union membership can be seen to fluctuate in the opposite direction to the business cycle. In times of relative prosperity, fear of losing one's job diminishes, and low unemployment gives workers the feeling that if they do lose their job, they could soon find another. In other words, economic growth may cause union decline. The UK has experienced economic growth since the 1990–92 recession, so this might explain the fall in membership. Conversely in a recession, unemployment is higher, and with fewer workers one might expect fewer union members; the cost of membership might also seem to be a deterrent if incomes are falling and it would seem logical that union numbers would fall in these circumstances. But in practice it seems that people hold on to their union membership when the economy is faltering.

Monopsony labour demand: the role of powerful employers

If trade unions sometimes seek to act as if there is a monopoly *supply* of labour, then looking at the market from a demand side, there might also be market domination in the *demand* for labour. If you lived in Brussels, for example, you would find that the combined effects of the European Commission and NATO headquarters have a large impact on wages of technically-minded workers. Pure monopsony exists where there is a **single buyer** of workers, although monopsony theory applies when there is any powerful buyer who can influence wages and employment levels: for example, the government is not the only buyer of doctors, but it has a strong voice in their pricing.

The theory MRP = MC is the same when MC is upward sloping, but MC is steeper than average cost (AC), meaning that one more worker (MC) will cost the firm *more* than the average wage (AC). When one more worker is employed, the wage has to be raised to attract the worker from another occupation. All the other workers will expect the same wage increase, so the marginal cost is much higher than the wage paid to get

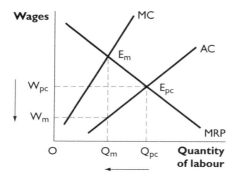

that last worker. Workers are willing to be employed up to the point where the last worker receives just enough to keep him or her in the current job (sometimes called the **transfer earnings**), and the wage (W_m) will be determined at Q_m (MRP = MC), where this equilibrium quantity corresponds with the AC curve. Wages and employment levels are below those in the competitive model (W_{pc}, Q_{pc}).

The disadvantages of monopsony

In a monopsony, it is easy to imagine a situation where employees are exploited by being paid the absolute minimum they need to stay in that job while the employer reaps all the profits. In the above diagram, you can see how the firm can exploit employees by paying them less than the full amount that they contribute to the value of output. Another disadvantage of monopsony is that workers in monopsony industries might leave the country. An example is the shortage of academics willing to remain in the universities in the UK — the so-called brain-drain. There may also be effects on productivity and 'added value' as workers gain little besides their wages from their work.

The advantages of monopsony

A firm needs to make a profit if it is to survive in the long run, and it can be argued that the lower wages that a worker earns in a monopsony provide a cushion of profits for the employer, making it more likely that the worker's job will be there in the long term. The profit made on each worker could be invested in capital to make the business more competitive in the long run. Another salient point is that employees' rights are now well enshrined in European law and an employee is no longer defenceless. For example, workers cannot be forced to work longer hours or in unsafe conditions, so even if firms are powerful, workers cannot be *exploited*.

To compare and contrast the effects of union and monopsony power, the following pair of diagrams can be used:

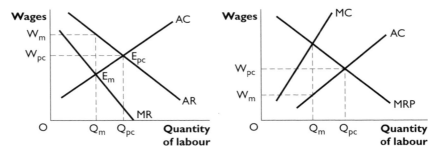

(a) Monopoly (trade unions) —
market power in supply of labour

(b) Monopsony (single employer) —
market power in demand for labour

Notice how, in diagram (a), wages are higher with a trade union than in the competitive model and employment is lower; and in diagram (b), the monopsony case, wages are lower and employment levels are also lower. Some people argue that if there were no unions, employment levels would be higher and if there were no monopsony power, again employment levels would be higher. This is not always true. For example, if trade unions work to *increase productivity* in line with wages, their existence will not cause employment to fall; and if monopsony power were reduced, there might still be enough profit within a firm to maintain employment levels.

Examination skills and concepts

- Trade union membership has stopped falling rapidly, and perhaps there is a new role for the unions, quite apart from collective bargaining.
- Changes in trade union or monopsony power can be analysed using diagrams, showing the effects on wages and employment levels.

Common examination errors

- Many candidates stray into politics when discussing trade unions, commenting on the 'death of socialism', for example, with the abandoning of Clause 4 (the part of the Labour Party constitution that made the unions powerful within the party), or the reduction in the relative value of benefits. Do not confuse this with evaluation — instead you should be looking to develop your *economic* arguments!

Useful exercises

- Sketch the monopoly and monopsony diagrams. Try to determine what happens at all the intersection points, and ask your teacher if you have got them right. If you can gain confidence in using the diagrams, you will not be afraid of using them under time pressure.
- Pencil in the changes in wages and employment levels if trade union or monopsony power were increased or decreased.

Links and common themes

- Market failure (Unit 2) introduces the idea of monopoly, and Unit 4 unravels the diagram. This is the only unit that deals with monopsony, and it adds a satisfying balance to the reasoning of uncompetitive markets.

Government intervention in labour markets in the UK and EU

This section looks at the implications of three pieces of legislation affecting labour markets in the UK and EU.

The Social Chapter

On its election in May 1997 the Labour government quickly adopted the Social Chapter of the Maastricht Treaty (1991). Until this time, the UK had exercised its right to 'opt out' of the Social Chapter, owing to fears that it would damage labour market flexibility in the UK. The Social Chapter sets out minimum requirements for parental leave, consultation rights and the role of works councils, and gives equal rights to part-time and fixed-term workers. The Working Time Directive, which was adopted by the UK in 1998, limits the number of hours per week that an employee can be required to work.

The UK has not yet felt the full effects of the Social Chapter, since some of the measures have not yet been implemented. At present, the UK labour market is still seen as much more flexible than those of France or Germany, but much less so than in the USA or Far East.

The national minimum wage

The national minimum wage (NMW) was introduced in 1999 at £4.10 per hour for anyone over the age of 21. Again, it was anticipated that this would cause problems in making labour markets too rigid and internationally uncompetitive. For example, Dyson moved its labour-intensive operations from Malmesbury in the UK to Malaysia largely on the basis of cheaper labour costs there. The following diagram may be used to show the competitive model.

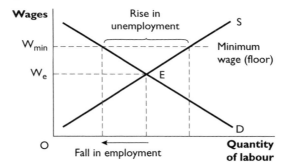

Effects of the national minimum wage on employment and unemployment

According to this model, the introduction of a minimum wage will cause a contraction along the demand curve and an expansion along the supply curve, resulting in unemployment. Most examination answers show the contraction in demand as firms find an alternative to labour or simply produce less; many forget to mention that, when there is a higher wage, there is an incentive for members of the inactive workforce to offer themselves for work. The fall in *employment* is, of course, smaller than the total effect on *unemployment*. So while those who are in work are better off, those who lose jobs or are out of the job market anyway are relatively worse off.

Why unemployment has not risen

The classical model has not been borne out in practice: indeed, unemployment has *fallen* since the introduction of the national minimum wage. There are several reasons for this:

- Firms do face a squeezing of their profits when their costs rise because of a rise in wages, but this does not always mean that they will make any workers redundant. This argument is based on the elasticity of demand for labour. Workers who are essential to the firm, such as cleaners in a restaurant, will not be laid off. Other ways will be found to cut costs.

- If workers produce a product that is not price-sensitive, an increase in their wages can be passed on to consumers as an increase in prices without much fall-off in demand, and therefore jobs are secure. This is the issue of price elasticity of demand for the final good.
- Advocates of the national minimum wage argue that paying workers a respectable wage makes them work harder and this increases the value of their output. If the wage is equal to the marginal revenue product, then a shift in the demand curve for labour could maintain employment levels or even increase them.
- It may just be a matter of the *level* of the NMW. In more highly paid regions of the UK it will have little impact — only 2% of workers in London are on the minimum wage, with equilibrium wages tending to be higher.

Why unemployment might yet rise

Many argue that, although the NMW has not as yet coincided with a rise in unemployment, this is simply a matter of time. Some reasons are as follows:

- The UK has had positive growth since the recession of 1990–92, and since 1995 has been outperforming many of its major trading partners. Firms have thus been able to sustain certain increases in costs because they can put up prices without losing revenue.
- Whereas in some industries a rise in costs can be sustained in the long run, many firms in the UK may become uncompetitive in the global market. It takes some time for buyers of UK goods to source cheaper alternatives, but it is argued that the demand will eventually move elsewhere, and UK unemployment will rise.
- The direct effect on many firms will be slight, particularly if they were not paying wages below the NMW anyway (for example, the lowest wage at McDonald's was £4.50 when the NMW was introduced). But there might be a knock-on effect in the long run as workers with higher skills or unsociable hours negotiate higher wages to maintain the *differential* between themselves and those on the minimum wage. As wages creep higher, the UK might gradually lose its competitive edge and jobs will go.

The impact of the NMW on income distribution

The NMW was designed to reduce poverty in the UK. For several reasons it can be said to be ineffectual:

- Although we might assume that the NMW affects those on lower incomes, in practice it often affects those who are second income earners, often part time. This might increase the welfare of these workers, but it will not reduce income inequalities between households.
- It does not affect workers under the age of 18, and those between the ages of 18 and 21 are paid at a lower level. The cost of living may be just as high for this latter age group and so this may be an unfair distinction.

- The unemployment trap occurs when the level of out-of-work benefits is higher than the amount that could be earned by going to work. The NMW theoretically reduces this trap and provides an incentive for people to go to work. The problem is that there still may not be any jobs available, and if those out of work cannot find gainful employment, income inequality will be widened and not narrowed.
- Elasticities of demand and supply tend to increase over time, which can be shown on a diagram by lowering the gradients of the demand and supply curves. Here the effect of the NMW is greater over time in increasing unemployment.
- Other things are not equal. The NMW might not rise as fast as inflation, in which case in real terms it would fall. The NMW does not reflect the purchasing power of a currency abroad, so changes in the exchange rate might affect relative poverty as spending power internationally is affected and the cost of living changes.

Equal pay

The Equal Pay Act (1970) essentially ruled that there should be the same pay for the same job. In practice this is not the case — hourly wages of women in the UK in 2003 are on average 82% of those of men, according to the Equal Opportunities Commission. There are economic and discriminatory reasons for this difference:

- **Human capital differences.** Historical differences in the levels of qualifications held by men and women have contributed to the pay gap. There may well be genuine differences between the average male and female worker — for example, relating to physical strength or psychological make-up — and women are still more likely than men to have breaks from paid work to care for children and other dependants. These breaks impact on women's level of work experience and therefore on their pay rates.
- **Part-time working.** The pay gap between men's and women's part-time hourly earnings and men's full-time hourly earnings is particularly large and, because so many women work part time, this is a major contributor to the gender pay gap. Some of this gap is due to part-time workers having lower levels of qualifications and less work experience. However, it is also due to part-time work being concentrated in less well-paid occupations.
- **Travel patterns.** On average, women spend less time commuting than men. This may be because of time constraints due to balancing work and caring responsibilities. This can impact on women's pay in two ways: a smaller pool of jobs to choose from and/or lots of women wanting work in the same location (near to where they live), leading to lower wages for those jobs. But much of the lack of female training or promotion stems from the fear that women might at some point leave for maternity reasons. From the woman's perspective, many need to find a job within their partner's area of work, so have less chance of promotion where it would require them to move with the job, or there may be fewer opportunities available.
- **Occupational segregation.** Female employment is highly concentrated in certain areas of work — 60% of working women work in just ten occupations — and those occupations that are female-dominated, such as cleaning, are often the lowest paid. In addition, women are still under-represented in the higher-paid jobs within

occupations. Think about your teachers at primary school: it is probable that most of the teachers were women but that the headteacher was male. High concentrations of female employees are associated with relatively low rates of pay. Higher levels of part-time working are also associated with lower rates of pay, even after other factors have been taken into account.

Other factors that affect the gender pay gap include: job grading practices, appraisal systems, reward systems and retention measures, wage-setting practices and, last but by no means least, discrimination.

Further important acts

- **Sex Discrimination Act (1975):** no differentials in pay based solely on gender or maternity issues — see **www.womenandequalityunit.gov.uk**
- **Employment Relations Act (1999):** fairness at work; right to join a trade union.
- **Race Relations Act (1976):** see the Equal Opportunities Commission website **www.eoc.org.uk**

On disability rights, see the Disability Rights Commission website: **www.drc-gb.org** For details of all UK legislation see **www.hmso.gov.uk**

Examination skills and concepts

- There is no need to learn the dates or factual content of these important acts — the key is to know their significance.
- When you visit the websites listed above, you will get a feel for the institutions, but again, don't think that you have to know everything. What is important is that you understand the role of various groups in protecting the workforce.

Common examination errors

- Many diagrams show correctly the contraction in demand when a minimum wage is introduced, but few show the expansion in supply, as more people are willing to work for the higher wage. The unemployment that results is *larger* than the fall in employment.

Unemployment

Anyone who is a member of the workforce but not currently working is said to be unemployed. In other words, the unemployed must be of working age and available as well as willing to work. These are the criteria in the UK for claiming Job-Seekers' Allowance (JSA). The claimant count, however, is not used internationally. One major weakness is that it does not always include the long-term unemployed because JSA can only be claimed for a 6-month stretch.

Since 1997 the official measure of unemployment has been the International Labour Organisation (ILO) measure. This method of defining the unemployed involves conducting surveys of a sample of the population, asking people whether they have

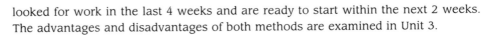

looked for work in the last 4 weeks and are ready to start within the next 2 weeks. The advantages and disadvantages of both methods are examined in Unit 3.

In October 2003 unemployment in the UK was 1.46 million, or 5% of the workforce, by the ILO measure (5.5% male, and women at the lowest ever figure of 4.3%). By the claimant count measure it was fairly stable at around 0.94 million, or 3.1%.

Types of unemployment

There are five major types of unemployment:

- **Frictional unemployment.** This measures the numbers in the workforce who are between jobs. It tends to increase in a boom rather than in a recession, unlike all the other types of unemployment. It is not seen as a problem because, by definition, in a flexible labour market, workers tend to be more mobile and can therefore move between jobs requiring the same skills without fear of long-term job loss.
- **Structural unemployment.** By contrast, when some industries contract and others expand and workers cannot move easily (they may be occupationally or geographically immobile), structural unemployment results. Structurally unemployed people lack the skills and training to take on new jobs. For example, coal miners do not easily become call operators.
- **Cyclical unemployment.** Throughout the stages of the business cycle unemployment varies, with a fall in unemployment when aggregate demand is high and vice versa. There may be a time lag. Firms are often reluctant to let go of workers when demand falls, for several reasons: first, they may have spent resources on training workers, which is a **sunk cost** (the investment cannot be recovered); second, they might have built up personal loyalties; third, they may expect a fall in demand to be shortlived and so may try to weather the downturn; and fourth, laying off workers involves redundancy packages that are enshrined in law, whereas it costs nothing to leave a machine unused except for the opportunity cost.
- **Seasonal unemployment.** The demand for agricultural workers is higher in the summer and the demand for sales assistants is higher at Christmas. There is little that can be done to change these patterns of demand for labour, but the main need is for these workers to be flexible so that they can get continued income flows throughout the year. Increasingly in the UK, the demand for seasonal labour is met by immigrant workers, or those working in the hidden economy.
- **Real-wage unemployment.** According to classical economists, this is the source of all unemployment except frictional. Wages are simply too high in some markets; if workers would accept lower wages, then more workers would have jobs. The process is that if one person wants a job that another already has, he or she may offer to do the job more cheaply. A rational employer will take the cheaper worker in the end, so long as the output is the same. This underbidding pushes wages down, as a newly unemployed worker will have to offer him or herself more cheaply. As the firms can now make more profit, they can take on more workers (see MRP theory on p. 19). One reason why wages might be too high is owing to minimum wage legislation, intended to reduce the unemployment trap which

occurs when a person is financially better off when not working. Higher wages make work worthwhile.

What can be done about unemployment?

- **Frictional unemployment.** The government's role must be to break down barriers for workers moving between jobs. This may mean, first, controlling the housing market (for example, allowing houses to be built where the jobs are in demand); second, giving tax breaks to firms providing training; and, third, improving information flows about job vacancies. In July 2003 the Deputy Prime Minister, John Prescott, announced a programme to build 200,000 new homes in the southeast for lower-paid workers; similarly, there has been an injection of cash into Job Centres to improve knowledge of the job market with modern technology.

- **Structural unemployment.** Here the emphasis must be on retraining, although in some cases this may take years because of heavy resistance. It is not clear that the advantages of retraining outweigh the disadvantages if workers are nearing the end of their working lives. However, in the future, with more than 40% of the population going to university, which arguably makes workers more occupationally flexible, and a higher level of skill required in manufacturing, structural unemployment may be expected to diminish.

- **Cyclical unemployment.** Many economists believe that the boom–bust cycle is no longer inevitable, largely owing to the independence of the Monetary Policy Committee in setting interest rates. It is certainly true that over the last 15 years the UK has had growth rates that have steadied. If the boom–bust cycle is indeed over, then this type of unemployment will cease to be a problem.

- **Seasonal unemployment.** As for frictional unemployment, the key is to increase flexibility.

- **Real-wage unemployment.** For those who believe that higher wages are causing unemployment, the answer is simple: cut wages wherever the supply of workers is greater than the demand. Psychologically this is a difficult process and may cause worker discontent, but in practice the same effect can be achieved if nominal wages rise more slowly than inflation: that is, if real wages fall. Another solution may be greater use of regional pay differences. There have, however, been many instances in the private sector where workers know that if they do not accept lower wages, they will lose their jobs. It is in the public sector (for example, among the firefighters) that resistance to wage reductions is likely to be more widespread. One of the solutions that the government has attempted is to force through increases in the productivity of the workforce so that productivity outstrips wage demands.

The duration and incidence of unemployment in the UK

A short period of unemployment is not thought to be harmful except in terms of income lost, for which there are safety nets in the UK in the form of income support. Unemployment becomes a problem when a worker becomes de-skilled. For example, a doctor who had been without a job for a long period would not know the latest developments in medicine and might therefore cause patients to receive second-best treatment. The problem of de-skilling varies depending on the type of job, but it is likely that the potential problem will be greater, the higher the skill involved. Other problems arising from long periods of unemployment concern the issue of morale, the social impact of having people out of work with little to do, relative poverty owing to the fact that benefits are low, and increased tax rates for those in work.

In the UK, the **incidence** of unemployment can be seen geographically with de-industrialisation in the midlands and north and the rapid growth of the service sector in the southeast. This has caused structural unemployment in areas where mining, shipbuilding, steel working and potteries used to predominate and some frictional unemployment in the still-growing service sector. The problems of social exclusion, community breakdown, poor health, crime and poor educational attainment prompted a large government investment in regeneration initiatives in the 1990s — see, for example, the work of the neighbourhood renewal unit at **www.renewal.net**

Ethnic unemployment is an important issue in the UK, where ethnic minority groups are more likely to be unemployed than whites possessing the same economic characteristics. This often reflects the age structure of different ethnic populations — those groups that might have extended family networks and higher percentages of older or younger people tend to have higher unemployment rates. UK residents of Pakistani and Bangladeshi origin suffer from unemployment three times higher (at 26%) than that of the white labour force. Indian groups are much less likely to be unemployed (12%), which may be explained by long-standing cultural ties, among other factors.

Examination skills and concepts
- Where supply of labour is greater than demand, there is unemployment. Wages are often sticky downwards — no one wants to have their wages cut, so unemployment can persist in the long run. This is called real-wage unemployment.
- Real-wage unemployment is thought by classical economists to be the main explanation of unemployment.
- The Keynesian approach is to accept that disequilibrium unemployment can persist in the long run.

Common examination errors
- Unequal pay between the sexes and ethnic groups is not always discrimination. For example, women may have less experience owing to family demands.

Useful exercises
- Draw up a table of reasons for unequal pay — one column for sound economic reasons, the other for discrimination.
- Look up the latest figures for unemployment in *Labour Market Trends* in the library or on the **www.statistics.gov.uk** website. Look at the regional changes and the changes by sex, part-time working and ethnic grouping.

Links and common themes
- This topic is an application of the unemployment theories learned in Units 3 and 6.

The changing structure and flexibility of the UK and EU labour markets

The *structure* of labour markets looks at demography (the study of population trends). *Flexibility* of labour markets measures the degree to which workers can adapt to firms' requirements — will workers accept lower wages, move location or retrain, or will they 'go slow', strike or dig their heels in if changes are imposed?

Ageing populations: the demographic time-bomb

A quick glance at the profile of the UK population shows that the average number of children per woman is falling and that people are living longer. Less obvious, perhaps, is the fact that women are choosing to have babies later in life (the average age of mothers on the arrival of their first baby is 30) and more women are expecting to return to their careers.

The working population has to support a greater number of those outside the working population, which is measured by the **dependency ratio**, the non-working population relative to the working population. In the UK the figure is just below 1:1.85. The dependency ratio is usually given as a decimal, which in the UK's case is 0.54 (1 divided by 1.85). The higher the decimal, the more people depend on the working population.

Another frequently used statistic is the old-age dependency figure (the number of people over retirement age divided by the working population), which in the UK is 0.24. In Italy the ratio is 0.29 (the highest in Europe). Projections show that the dependency ratio will increase markedly in the future — hence the term 'demographic time-bomb'.

In the short run, a falling birth-rate means that there are more women in the working population, but it is only a matter of time before there are grave shortages of people of working age and a huge increase in the number of those beyond retirement age.

The impact of an ageing population

The specification asks candidates to look at the impact of ageing populations on two aspects of the economy: labour markets and governments.

Labour markets

- Workers will not be able to expect the government to provide for them after retirement. The gap between pensions and incomes is likely to increase. This means that workers will need to put more money into private pension schemes, which will affect their incentives at work.
- Tax rates can be expected to rise, therefore reducing incentives.

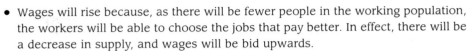

- Wages will rise because, as there will be fewer people in the working population, the workers will be able to choose the jobs that pay better. In effect, there will be a decrease in supply, and wages will be bid upwards.
- Real-wage unemployment is likely to fall. With supply contracting it is unlikely that wages will be too high in any industry.
- Product markets will change, which will feed through to labour markets. For example, fewer nursery workers will be required (their wages will fall in relative terms) but more care-home workers will be needed (their wages will increase).

Governments

- Falling tax revenues and increased government spending will necessitate higher tax take. Whether this will mean an increase or a decrease in tax rate may be analysed using the Laffer curve. The Laffer curve shows the effect on total tax revenue of changing tax rates. Tax revenue is zero when tax rates are 0% or 100%, and rises to a peak somewhere between the two. You can use the Laffer curve to show that, when cutting very high tax rates, you could get people to work longer hours and pay more tax in total.
- A sector where the government will spend more is likely to be healthcare, while nursery provision is likely to receive less. The government might also, in the medium term, use subsidies to encourage women with children back to work.
- Retirement ages may be raised; indeed, 'compulsory' retirement ages may be phased out. Initiatives are likely to be introduced to make work more flexible.

Changing participation rates

The participation rate refers to the number of people who are economically active as a proportion of the population of working age. It includes those who are in employment (employees or self-employed) and those who are not in employment but who are actively seeking work.

Factors affecting the size, age and sex distribution of the supply of labour

In September 2003 the labour force was 29 million, out of a total population of working age of 46 million, making the **participation rate** 63%; 15.8 million are males (participation rate 70.9%) and 13.4 million are females (participation rate 55.6%). The male participation rate has fallen from 81% over the last 30 years, and the female participation rate has risen from 44%. The gap between the genders is therefore getting closer.

In June 2003 the **employment rate** was 74.7%. This is the proportion of those in work relative to those of working age, of which 15 million are male and 12.8 million female. If unemployment is only 5% it means that around 20% of the working-age population are not willing to work, i.e. they are economically inactive. About 1.9 million males are part time compared to 6.1 million females; the fact that four-fifths of part-timers are female indicates that women continue to take on the traditional roles of childcare and 'home working'.

The labour force is also getting older. Twenty years ago, 46% of workers were aged between 16 and 34, compared to around 42% now.

The factors that determine these changes are demographics (population changes), social factors (women returning to work, having fewer babies), technology (working from home may mean that childcare can be shared by the sexes, for example) and tradition (women are not allowed to do paid work in some religions, for example).

Migration

Owing to enormous skill shortages in the UK, governments have used many strategies to try to attract highly skilled immigrants. Given that these people find long-term jobs, this is likely to improve the flexibility and income distribution within the country. However, most UK immigrants tend to be asylum seekers, who, although possibly skilled, may not have skills that match the jobs available. In this case, wages of low-skilled workers are likely to be bid downwards. Furthermore, in the informal economy, wages might fall very low for illegal immigrants.

An alternative solution to skill shortages is **outsourcing**, where foreign workers do not physically move country, but may be fully employed by UK firms, a process made increasingly possible by broadband access to the internet. For example, British Airways uses technical staff living in Mumbai to process its ticketing. The Indian workforce may cost as little as one-tenth the wages of the UK workforce.

The problems of a **dual labour market** (when there is a two-speed system of advancement in the economy) often follow from the immigration of low-skilled workers. In the fast lane there is equality of opportunity for all, and workers can all progress up a career structure. In the slow lane, low skills mean little training or other opportunities to develop. Immigrants are often stuck firmly in the slow lane. As with the glass ceiling (see p. 23), some of the reasons for this are economic (e.g. language as a barrier to entry), but others result from pure prejudice.

Examination skills and concepts
- Dependency ratios indicate the number of dependants relative to the number in the working population. In the EU these figures are set to rise by 76% by 2050.
- A time-bomb is one that explodes after a certain period has passed. The demographic time-bomb is due to explode in the 2020s in the UK, when the baby boomers (the postwar never-had-it-so-good high birth rate generation that came to an end in the early 1960s with the onset of the contraceptive pill) have all retired.
- Participation ratios show the number of those willing to work relative to those of working age. If you go to university, you will be lowering the participation ratio in the short run, although the long-term benefits to the economy are likely to be greater.

Common examination errors
- Those who are unemployed are still in the working population. If you are asked to give ways of increasing participation ratios and talk about ways of cutting unemployment, such as reducing the Job-Seeker's Allowance, you are unlikely to earn marks.

Links and common themes
- The Laffer curve may be looked at in detail under fiscal policy in Unit 6.

Income and wealth

Income is a **flow** concept — the receipt of resources that is repeated over time. It includes not only wages, but also dividends from shares, or rent on a property.

Wealth is a **stock** concept — something that you own. Around one-quarter of the wealth in the UK is held in the form of property, another quarter in share and pension-fund ownership and the rest in the many other forms of monetary and physical assets.

Inequality exists when there is a large gap between the top earners and bottom earners (using income as a measure) or when the assets of the rich are contrasted with those of the poor (using wealth as a measure).

The issues relating to income and wealth that may be brought up on the exam paper are the factors that influence the distribution of income and wealth, and the changes that may occur as a result of government policy.

Distribution of income and wealth

Supporters of the capitalist system generally believe that a degree of inequality is a good thing — the desire to earn or have more makes people work harder and makes them more careful with the resources that they have. However, while there is no agreement as to how equal incomes and wealth should be, most people agree that a huge degree of inequality must be harmful for those at the bottom end of the spectrum.

Measuring income inequality

The degree of income inequality can be measured using the **Lorenz curve**.

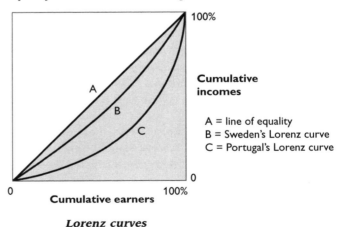

Lorenz curves

If everybody earned the same, there would be a perfectly even distribution of income (although not necessarily of wealth). This is shown by the straight line across the chart, which maps the cumulative income against the cumulative population. Although this is a fair distribution, it could never happen in practice because all humans have individual characteristics and skills that will earn different wages, as explained in the section on wage determination (pp. 21–24). The further the Lorenz curve moves from the line of equality, the more uneven the distribution of income will be.

The degree of inequality is measured by the **Gini coefficient**, the ratio of the area between the Lorenz curve and the line of equality relative to the shaded triangle. The higher the figure for the Gini coefficient, the greater is the degree of inequality between higher- and lower-income households. A value of zero indicates that each earner receives an equal share of income. At the other extreme, a value of 1 shows perfect inequality in income distribution. Examples of countries with high Gini coefficients are India and Saudi Arabia, where the majority of income is earned by a tiny minority of the population. In Sweden the coefficient is very low and a higher proportion of the population earns the majority of income.

The **income gap** between rich and poor is best measured using disaggregated data, such as **deciles:** deciles are 10% of a cumulative frequency. There will always be a bottom 10% of incomes — the issue is how large the gap is between the bottom earners and, say, the middle earners. Similarly, we can measure inequality as a whole by measuring the gap between the bottom 10% and the top 10%.

Another method of assessing inequality is by measuring **poverty**. There are two ways to do this:
- **Absolute poverty** measures the number of people below a certain sustainable rate of income, i.e. those who live on less than, say, £120 per week in the UK. This is an arbitrary figure, based on what is thought to be enough to live on. Very few people in the UK live in absolute poverty, when compared globally or over time.
- **Relative poverty** measures the gap between the bottom deciles of income and the higher deciles. A poverty line is drawn relative to the average income: for example, those people on less than 60% of average income might be defined as poor. There is a major problem with this measure — the poverty line shifts with average incomes, and it is difficult to judge the performance of governments, let alone set out policies. If economic growth is shared equally by all (in percentage terms), then poverty by this measure will automatically increase!

Income inequality in the UK
In the UK, the income gap has widened since Labour came to power in 1997, returning to levels last seen at the end of the economic boom of the 1980s. In the short run, economic growth usually benefits the higher income groups primarily, and therefore widens income differentials. Under Thatcher, the inequality gap widened — the poorest gained very little from the late 1980s boom. Under Major, there was little economic growth, but the poorest did gain relatively.

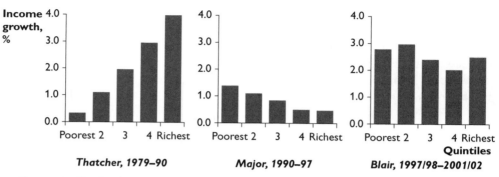

Thatcher, 1979–90   *Major, 1990–97*   *Blair, 1997/98–2001/02*

Source: A. Shephard (2003) *Inequality Under the Labour Government,* Institute of Fiscal Studies Briefing Note No. 33

Real yearly income growth by income quintile, 1979–2002

Under Blair, there has been strong income growth, and the Gini coefficient reached a peak in 2000 of 0.35. Since then there have been signs of a slight decline, narrowly closing the income gap. Many explain this by the New Deal and Welfare to Work strategies, together with a switch towards greater means testing for benefit recipients, thus directing benefit payments to the poorest.

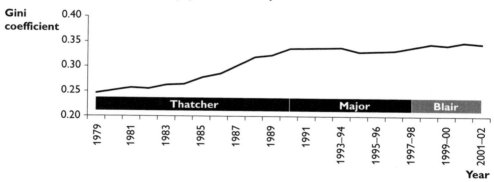

Note: incomes are measured before housing costs and adjusted for family size.
Source: Family Resources Survey and Family Expenditure Survey

The Gini coefficient

Factors influencing the distribution of income and wealth

- **Inheritance.** One quarter of wealth in the UK is in the form of property, which passes through families. As property prices rise, the distribution of wealth becomes wider between those who have property and those who do not.
- **Age.** Older and more experienced workers can often command higher wages, although during the dotcom bubble of the late 1990s the reverse seemed to be true. Older workers benefit from accumulated wealth and possibly reduced expenditure on housing and education. We sometimes refer to the 'grey pound' of older generations whose disposable income is greater.

- **Education.** Recent policy changes regarding university tuition fees and the 'graduate tax' (where fees and loans are repaid through higher taxes after leaving college) reflect the inequality of income between those with and without a higher education. The government has ruled that those without such an education should not be expected to subsidise the tuition of those who will gain from it in the long run. Why should a postal worker pay for the training of a solicitor? An alternative would be to make the income tax system more progressive, which would have a similar effect as a graduate tax because graduates are likely to be in the higher tax bands.
- **Pensions.** There are two major types of private pension, one related to final salaries and one based on the value of contribution, often in relation to the stock market. Final salary pensions have proved to be unsustainable for employers in times of stock market uncertainty (2002–03), so these have largely been abandoned by firms. The second type of pension causes great uncertainty and can leave some pensioners unable to maintain their standard of living. There is also a state pension provided by the government — for those who have no other means of support this will be their only source of income. In real terms, this is falling owing to the UK's ageing population (see pp. 37–38).
- **State benefits and expenditures.** The UK government has traditionally offered state benefits that are judged to be sufficient to provide a decent standard of living. However, certain governments have tried to keep down benefits to give poorer people a greater incentive to find other sources of income. The UK has a progressive income tax system which means that as wages go up, so do marginal tax rates: extra income over a certain threshold is taxed at a higher rate. The system therefore takes more money as a percentage from higher income earners than from lower income earners, and this revenue can then be used to subsidise the poor.
- **Property and stock market prices.** These are major factors in the distribution of wealth in the UK. Historically, house prices and stock market prices have moved in the same direction, although the early part of this decade saw a rapid rise and fall in stock market prices which has not as yet been mirrored in the housing market. Rising asset prices increase inequality in the distribution of wealth.

Government policy

Government policy has influenced the distribution of income and wealth in a number of ways over the last 10 years.

The tax and benefit system
- The major change has been to increase the number of bands of income taxation.
- Inheritance tax and stamp duty have become graduated so that the wealthier are taxed more.
- Working Families Tax Credit has been introduced to smooth over problems at the lower end of incomes and the top level of benefits, which addresses the problems of the unemployment and poverty traps.
- A means-tested Child Tax Credit, introduced in 2003, benefits those who work and have children, and replaces the married person's tax allowance.

- The child benefit scheme remains largely unchanged in structure: it is totally unrelated to income — even the prime minister and his wife get it — and it is paid per child up to the age of 18. Recent increases in child benefit are not going to reduce income inequalities greatly.
- State pensions have been declining in real terms, which widens the income gap. The furore resulting from the 75p state pension increase in 2000 (which was based on the retail price index in September of that year) has forced the government to consider raising pensions in line with average incomes rather than inflation. But this is a costly option, and current workers are now being strongly encouraged to buy private pension schemes on top of the state provision.
- In terms of benefits, it has been made harder to claim the 'dole' or Job-Seeker's Allowance, and the stigma attached to claiming all kinds of benefits discourages many of the very poor from making a claim. The non-collection of benefits is a serious problem for the government.
- Means-testing benefits is a policy favoured by the current chancellor, although non-collection will work against the redistributive intentions. Specific means-tested benefits recently introduced are Child Tax Credit and Working Families Tax Credit, described above.

Non-tax and benefit methods of income redistribution
- The introduction of the national minimum wage (see pp. 30–32) was one attempt to reduce poverty in the UK.
- Introduced in 1998, the New Deal programme offers a package to the young unemployed, whereby they can receive benefits only if they undertake training. Firms are supported by subsidy in reward for taking on these low-skill workers, in respect of their often-low productivity rates (output per head).
- Other training schemes are being devised — on-the-job training for teachers, for example, and vocational A-levels. The proposed introduction of the baccalaureate to replace A-levels will include a compulsory element of vocational skills and foreign languages for all 16–18-year-olds. It is hoped that this will make young people more productive in the workplace, and improve the flexibility of workers within the EU. Even if these effects are realised without lost skills elsewhere, there will be a significant time lag.

Examination skills and concepts
- Being able to use the Lorenz curve to illustrate inequality: if the bottom 10% earn a very small percentage of the income, the curve will be a long way from the line of equality (the Gini coefficient will be high), and the top 10% will earn a very large percentage of the income.
- Learn more from the website **www.ifs.org.uk** which has clear explanations and applications of this.

Common examination errors
- Confusing income distribution policies (e.g. changing the bands of income tax) with wealth distribution policies (such as inheritance tax) and expenditure taxes (such as VAT).

- Lack of clarity in defining inequality and poverty.
- Bias to the poor. While you might feel strongly about certain social issues, you must present the range of views, and try to illustrate what problems governments face in dealing with the issues. There are no obvious solutions or they would have been tried.

Useful exercises

- Draw a diagram of the economy where the stock of wealth is the water in a bathtub, income is water from the taps and expenditure is the escape of water via the plug hole. Use the concept to show how income and wealth are related: the bath water level can be at an equilibrium or changing; you could have two sources of income; show how you could have a very high income but no wealth; you could even put in a water pump to represent the production units, and add leakages from the pipes.

Links and common themes

- Income and wealth in Unit 3 is a useful starting point, but the issues must be related to the workforce.
- The fiscal policy issues in Units 3 and 6 are important. It would be helpful to consider the macroeconomic effects of changes in, say, the tax and benefit system, and then relate this back to the labour market via incentives or UK competitiveness and therefore unemployment.

Questions
&
Answers

This section contains six data-response questions designed to be used as part of your learning and exam preparation. In the 90 minutes available for the exam, you should take about 15 minutes to read and choose from two such questions on the paper. There is nothing worse than getting half way through a question and realising that you would have been able to respond better to the other question.

This section also includes:

- a student answer varying between grade A and grade C to each question
- examiner's comments on each answer, explaining, where relevant, how the answer could be improved. These comments are preceded by the icon *e*.

Question 1

The European context

Until about 1990 there were no serious concerns about Italian economic performance. The wealth generated by companies such as the Fiat group pulled the whole economy along. There were legitimate worries about the distribution of that wealth and in particular about the gap between the north and the south — parts of northern Italy are richer than much of Britain. But despite this, the overall numbers were impressive.

But there is now a growing concern that growth is no longer sustainable. While the country was industrialising rapidly, with a large supply of labour coming off the land and moving north, it could achieve high growth rates. Once that process tailed off, the growth engine ground to a halt. Companies that had been slow to adapt, like the car division of Fiat, found they had little comparative advantage in a harsher world.

Now, there are several unusual features to the Italian economy. One is that the number of hours worked is relatively low, but more remarkable is the low labour participation rate: less than 60% of the people of working age are in jobs or at least looking for them, compared with 63% in the UK. You could say that the country manages to achieve a high standard of living — as well as a high quality of life — without having to work too hard. Many would find that a rather attractive combination — if it were sustainable. Sadly, I fear it is not.

You can see why in the two graphs, which come from United Nations population estimates. Figure 1 shows the likely changes in population for selected countries over the next half-century. Even if you take those with a pinch of salt, which you should with all such projections, there is a prospect of Italy losing a significant proportion of its population.

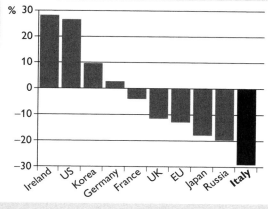

Figure 1 Population projections: % change in population 2000–50

data-response question 1

The reason for this is shown in Figure 2, which gives estimated total fertility rates for 1995–2000. Italy has the lowest of the G7 and vies with Spain to be bottom of the EU league. Italians are said to love children — they just don't have very many of them.

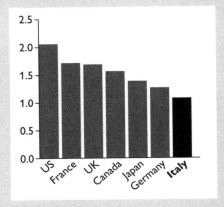

Figure 2 Total fertility rates: average number of children born per woman

If there is indeed to be a bout of economic reform in Italy, the country will be better placed to start growing again. But it will only grow briskly if it wants to. The danger is that the brightest young Italians will look elsewhere for jobs. For example, Italy happens to produce very good economists, many of whom have come to Britain. Were outward migration to rise, the population decline would become even more serious.

Source: Hamish McRae, 'Arrivederci, la dolce vita', *Independent*, 26 January 2003.

(a) **Assess policy options available to a government that has 'legitimate worries about the distribution of…wealth…between the north and the south'.** (15 marks)

(b) **Using demand and supply analysis, discuss the possible reasons why the 'number of hours worked is relatively low' in Italy.** (20 marks)

(c) **Evaluate two policies that the Italian government might use to increase the size of the working population.** (15 marks)

(d) **Assess the impact of migration on the Italian labour market.** (10 marks)

■ ■ ■

Candidate's answer

(a) One problem in Italy is geographical immobility. Workers cannot easily move to where there are well-paid jobs available. There may be cultural reasons why people cannot move — language problems (local dialects) or housing problems. This causes labour market inflexibility, so wages are higher in some locations than in others. The government could help with providing finance for new homes, offer training schemes for language and improve information flows so that people know what jobs are available.

The government could use the tax and benefit system to help the poor and redistribute money from the rich. It might make income tax more progressive, or increase inheritance taxes. In the UK a tiered system of inheritance tax has been introduced to tax the wealthy more heavily. And stamp duty is stepped so that houses that cost more than certain amounts have to pay a higher tax.

4/15 marks

e The student has made a classic mistake and written mostly about income and not wealth. The two concepts are closely related, but the connection must be made explicit. All of the marks here are awarded for the final analysis on wealth taxes. Note that you don't need to know anything factually about Italy. The candidate has made many valid points, which would be true for any EU country.

(b) The shape of the supply curve is determined by the income and substitution effects. While the substitution effect is always positive — the more money offered, the higher the opportunity cost of work — the income effect can switch the other way. The text implies that in Italy the living standard is high, so people can afford to work less and enjoy leisure time. So a strong income effect might mean that people do not offer themselves for many hours of work, even when wages seem very attractive.

A second reason why supply might be low is a highly progressive tax. If marginal tax rates rise with income, there is little incentive to work more hours. For example, I work in a pizza café on Saturdays. I don't pay any tax because I earn less than the personal allowance (around £4,500). If I had paid work for the rest of the week, I probably wouldn't do the Saturdays because I would have to pay tax. The extra work is taxed, so I'm less likely to do it.

A third reason why supply is low might be because of powerful unions. They might restrict supply in order to keep wages up. In the UK, the Musicians' Union stops its members from taking jobs below a certain rate of pay, which is well above the equilibrium wage. This means they must work fewer hours because the concert organisers can't afford the higher fees, so don't put on the concerts. These are a merit good and people are not willing to pay what they really cost — as with all the arts, in fact.

11/20 marks

e You need to give four factors for a 20-mark question. It is encouraging to see the use of anecdotal evidence, but don't go on and on about an issue, even if you do feel strongly about it. A brief word about the Musicians' Union closed shop might be in order, but this answer is going very much astray by treading into Unit 2 territory. While this is not actually penalised in any way, you are unlikely to be focused on the question if you are using material solely from another unit or indeed another A-level subject. A diagram would easily earn analysis marks in response to this question.

(c) It could encourage immigration. Immigrants are likely to be of working age. They are also likely to be keen to work — that's why they moved there. However, there

ata-response question 1

may be language problems, so they may become dependants rather than earners. And they may bring large families with them.

A second policy could be to increase the cost of university tuition. This is being attempted in the UK — by introducing top-up fees the government is putting people off going to university, and instead they might try to find a job. In the short run this will increase the GDP and reduce the costs of higher education for the government, but in the long run this is clearly disastrous. The population will have lower skills and crime rates might rise. Those who do go to university will have bigger loans, so they are going to have to work in pubs etc. during the week, which will lower the quality of their education. **9/15 marks**

e The candidate has correctly identified the concept of the working population — those who are at work or are offering themselves for work. The policy options chosen are not the most obvious, and the evaluation might have emphasised that other policies, such as Working Families Tax Credit, might have a greater and more direct impact on the working population.

The candidate's handling of the tuition fees issue contains much apparent evaluation, although what is presented is heated debate rather than clearly rational arguments. There needs to be more analysis about how this actually works. And you might remember that not *all* education is effective in increasing the skills of the workforce. The aim of government intervention should be made clear, that is, to reduce income inequalities rather than to reduce student numbers.

(d) Migration is the movement of people across borders. These will not always be members of the working population, but it is likely that there will be one potential income earner in each family unit that migrates and this may well be the motivation for them moving.

The passage states that the brightest young Italians are the most likely to leave Italy. These workers are likely to be highly productive in the Italian economy — they would contribute a high value added. The ever-increasing ageing population in Italy needs productive workers to support them. The loss of these workers would have a multiplier effect — the knock-on effects would be much greater as aggregate demand shrinks — and this could affect the labour market, as workers are made redundant.

If there is emigration of skilled workers, there may be labour shortages in some areas. Either the country won't be able to produce at such high levels or there will be widening wage differentials — there may even be a dual economy as the fast track excludes the unskilled. This decrease in supply puts up wages and reduces employment.

However, labour might be leaving the country because there aren't suitable jobs in the domestic economy. The passage refers to economists — maybe these workers will reach higher wage levels and status by leaving the country. The incentive and the freedom to do so might encourage more people to train, and as wages continue to rise, workers will be attracted *into* Italy. The single European market means that there is freedom of movement between countries. While there will be a long time lag, you would still expect an increase in supply as wages and opportunities have risen, although language and cultural barriers may persist into the long run.

10/10 marks

e This answer is focused and applied, and there is plenty of analysis. The candidate evaluates both short- and long-run effects. Another way of earning the evaluation marks might have been to refer to the issues of 'brain drain' as much on the negative side as on the positive. However, the answer would earn full marks because all of the required elements are present, even if the flow of the prose is not perfect.

Scored 34/60 = grade C

Question 2

Demand, supply and wage determination in the construction industry

For those who draw comfort from the idea that everything in life is worse than it used to be, there is good news. Plumbers really are harder to come by and costlier than they once were. Regrettably, however, the declining morals of the British working man may not be to blame. A construction boom and government education policy are likelier culprits.

After a slump in construction in the early 1990s, which reduced the workforce from 1.8 million in 1990 to 1.4 million in 1996, the industry has recovered and the workforce has grown by about 100,000. Steady growth has turned to boom, and in 2001 construction grew by 3.5%, faster than the economy generally for the first time since 1989. The resulting labour shortages have been pushing up pay rates, particularly in southeast and southwest England. According to one building firm in south London, in 2000 a plumber cost £120 a day and a bricklayer £100; this year, a plumber costs £230, and a bricklayer £180.

This problem is likely to get worse. The industry is said to be likely to grow by about 4.5% this year and about 4% next. Even at a lower growth rate of 2.6%, the Construction Industry Training Board (CITB) reckons that the industry needs to recruit 76,000 people a year rather than the 45,000 trainees it currently gets.

Why, when the pay is so good, is it so hard to recruit people? The industry has not had a particularly good image. Quite apart from jokes about builders with jeans halfway down their bums, stories of cowboy builders and poor safety records on construction sites discourage the self-respecting young.

Another problem is the government's enthusiasm to send more people to university. Andy Watts, chief executive of the Institute of Plumbing, reckons that Tony Blair's target of getting 50% of 18–30-year-olds into university by 2010 is a big mistake. 'It sends all the wrong signals to young people who are not that gifted,' he says.

The government is, however, starting to steer more middle-grade pupils into training for construction jobs, by introducing vocational A-levels and putting more money into further education colleges. The CITB is trying to change the construction industry's image by recruiting in schools and through magazines targeted at fashionable young things, such as *Loaded* and *Cosmopolitan*. The ads suggest that if you want to be your own boss, have plenty of money and create something real, then building might be a cool job. It seems to be paying off: the CITB says that applications for apprentice-ships are 30% up this year, and registrations for plumbing courses are up by 50%.

Even so, more carpenters and plumbers will not emerge for some years yet: the way the training works in Britain, it takes 4 years to qualify as a plumber. This is a big headache all round. The government's spending splurge on new hospitals and schools means that the industry expects public sector construction output to rise by more than 8% this year and next, and by 6% in 2004 compared with an average growth of only 1.2% in the last 3 years. Labour shortages mean not only that the cost of these projects will be more than forecast, but also that, as craftsmen are sucked into public sector work, it will be even harder to get that plumber for some time to come.

Source: '"Sorry mate, too busy" — why you can't get a plumber', *The Economist*, 23 November 2002.

(a) Using evidence from the passage, discuss the shape of the likely supply curve for plumbers. (10 marks)
(b) Using demand and supply analysis, examine the factors that have led to the increase in wages for plumbers since 2000. (15 marks)
(c) To what extent can the market for plumbers be said to be competitive? (20 marks)
(d) Assess the impact on the labour market of the 'target of getting 50% of 18–30-year-olds into university by 2010'. (15 marks)

■ ■ ■

Candidate's answer

(a) Two effects can explain the shape of the supply curve: as wages rise, there will be a substitution effect and an income effect. The substitution effect is the factor that as more money is offered, more work is done. If a person has two trades, plumbing and plastering, then as the plumbing wages go up he will be more likely to do plumbing jobs. The substitution effect is likely to be fairly weak as wages rise — many construction workers have specialised skills and are unlikely to be able to pick and choose the jobs that pay the best. This would make the supply curve fairly inelastic. In addition, it takes a long time (4 years) to train to be a plumber, as it says in the final paragraph, which makes the substitution effect even weaker.

The income effect describes the effect on plumbers when they have the extra money — do they offer more work, or do they make do on the higher-paid jobs and keep the average homeowner waiting, as described in the passage? This is likely to become a stronger effect as wages rise, so much so that the supply curve might even bend backwards as plumbers take longer holidays on the higher incomes. The combined effect can be illustrated as follows.

data-response question 2

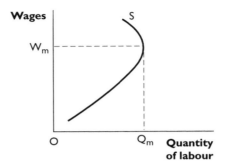

9/10 marks

📝 This is a good attempt at the theory. The candidate mentions the passage explicitly, and the analysis is secure. The use of elasticity shows the *extent* of the impact on wages, and thus earns evaluation marks. To improve, the candidate should have come to a justified conclusion — for example, that because of low price elasticity of supply, an increase in demand, as mentioned in the passage, will have a large effect on wages.

(b) The demand for plumbers is a derived demand — it is determined by the demand for buildings. The demand for construction has increased because of the public demand for houses and also the government's demand for schools and hospitals. This causes the demand curve for labour to shift outwards.

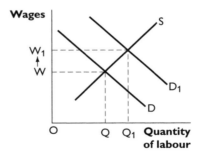

The supply of plumbers has fallen because of government education policy. The supply curve shifts to the left.

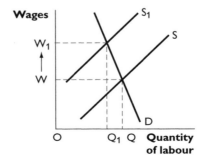

The shift in supply has a large effect on wages because the demand for plumbers is inelastic. There is no substitute, and the proportion of total construction costs spent on plumbing is relatively small. This is shown in the above diagram by the steep demand curve — wages move more than employment. If you need a plumber, you'll pay for one! **8/15 marks**

e This is an average answer. When making reference to the data, the candidate should have mentioned the specific detail in the passage (the second and the final paragraphs for the demand shift, and the fifth paragraph for supply). There will be line numbers in the passage in the exam, so that your reference can be even more specific.

When the candidate refers to the elasticity of demand for plumbers, the answer is starting to evaluate. The concept is used to show the *extent* to which the shift in demand affects the wages. The candidate could have gone further: the elasticity of supply is also very low — the passage refers to the 4 years' training required. This will have the effect of further pushing up wages when the demand curve shifts to the right.

Another successful way to evaluate here would have been to refer to monopsony power. The government is described in the passage as being a major employer, and its power in the market leaves smaller employers in a weak bargaining position: if they want to employ a plumber, they may have to pay 'over the odds' to entice workers away from secure, long-term employment with the government. This application of market failure would earn evaluation marks.

(c) Government demand pushes out the demand curve for labour. This is likely to increase wages and employment levels. This is the allocation of scarce resources (plumbers) to those buyers who are prepared to pay for them (government). The government is not a true monopsony because many firms and private individuals also buy labour. But as a big player in the market, the government is likely to be able to influence wages and will get the plumbers more easily. The government has market power, and because it offers a lot of work and is more likely to offer long-term prospects, plumbers are likely to be attracted to this work. So it may be able to pay less — public sector wages are often below private sector wages for this reason.

The supply of labour is also uncompetitive. The CITB has an impact on the supply of labour through its advertising campaigns. This implies that there is not perfect knowledge in the market for plumbers, and that people can be influenced to train if they are told that it's 'cool'. This implies that there is asymmetric information in this market — the people who could train to be plumbers do not realise what they would gain out of it. **16/20 marks**

e This is an A-grade answer: there is evaluation on both the demand and supply side. However, the candidate could have spelt out the case that there is competition in the demand and supply of labour in the long run. For example, on the supply side, with the single European market since 1993, plumbers can move freely around Europe.

data-response question 2

(d) In the short run the labour market will decrease, as fewer people are offering themselves for work. Tax rates might increase too, because most of the fees are paid by government (at the moment!). This might make people less inclined to work, and the attractiveness of leisure time increases.

In the long run, the newly qualified graduates will be more flexible, it is thought, and they will have skills that will increase their MRP. This increase in the demand for labour makes UK workers more attractive internationally, and there might be an impact on quality of output.   **9/15 marks**

This answer is brief but effective because the time factor is included. Try to avoid making your answers too personal or political, and stick to the impact on the *labour* market when explicitly requested to do so.

Score 42/60 = grade A

Question 3

The unions and the Working Time Directive

Extract 1: Time is money

Whatever their posturing, union leaders and ministers know that Britain's workplace is now shaped far more in Brussels than in London. A tide of European laws is succeeding where UK unions failed, in giving more rights to employees. These gains come at a cost not just to employers but also to taxpayers as the economy generates less output.

Since the end of 1999, for example, parents have enjoyed new rights to take time off when they have a young child. Fathers have been able to insist on this for the first time and mothers also get extra time with young children over and above maternity leave. Both become eligible to this right to parental leave after working with their employer for no more than a year.

European directives are also granting workers new rights to be informed and consulted on what their employers are planning, especially with regard to employment. Since the start of 2000, large multinationals have had to comply in Britain with a law establishing European works councils. Any firm with more than 150 staff will from 2005 also have to inform and consult its workers about its business and employment prospects. Trade unions hope — and employers fear — that this will become a platform for the unions to claw back recognition in private sector workplaces, where less than a fifth of employees are members.

Other European legislation has given part-time and fixed-term contract workers the right to be treated as favourably as comparable full-time employees. The EU is also planning to confer new rights on agency staff, so that after 6 weeks they enjoy the same rights at work, including pay, as comparable employees in the companies where they are temping.

But the law with the greatest effect on firms is the Working Time Directive, passed as a health and safety measure to create a level playing field in the single European market, which restricts the average working week to a 48-hour maximum. The impact on employers and the economy has been substantial. According to the British Chambers of Commerce, the directive is costing employers £2.3 billion a year. Although there are a number of exemptions, it has had a clear effect on the average number of hours worked per employee (see Figure 1). This has dropped by nearly 3% since the directive became law in 1998, even though the economy has grown respectably over most of this period.

data-response question 3

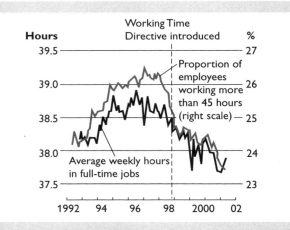

Figure 1   Clocking off: the impact of the Working Time Directive

The Treasury argues that the effect of the directive has now largely run its course. But this seems unlikely. For one thing, the directive will be extended over the next few years to cover transport workers and junior doctors. For another, individuals can at present opt out of the 48-hour limit on the working week, but this is now under review.

With 4 million employees continuing to work more than 48 hours a week, there is plenty of scope for the directive to cut time at work still further. This will reduce economic growth. Employment rights sound fine but they are costly not just to employers but also to the wider economy.

Source: adapted from *The Economist*, 14 September 2002.

Extract 2: The trade union perspective

What I would conclude from the trends is that union decline has most to do with the changing economic and industrial structure of the country, rather than workers walking away from unions.

Our problems are rooted in the decline of unionised workplaces — both their absolute number and the number of people they employ — and our failure to organise in many new workplaces. Even in sectors like manufacturing where unionisation is common, it tends to be older workplaces that are unionised — and newer ones that are not.

The legal changes made by the Conservative government were damaging to unions and to people at work, but our membership fell more because of their economic policies than their legal changes. Many of these trends have continued unabated since the 1980s. In particular, in recent years there have been huge losses of manufacturing jobs — and often in the older unionised sectors such as textiles.

Yet our membership has now stopped falling. That is a significant achievement. Something must be going right for us. And indeed it is. There are a number of factors working in our favour.

Source: Brendan Barber, TUC General Secretary, **www.city.ac.uk** (City University website), September 2003.

(a) **Discuss the impact on wages and employment levels of the shift in the supply of labour, which results from the introduction of the Working Time Directive in the UK.** (15 marks)

(b) **Assess the argument that European laws are succeeding where trade unions failed.** (20 marks)

(c) **Evaluate the possible effects of the Working Time Directive on income distribution and labour market flexibility.** (10 marks)

(d) **Examine the implications of the decline in trade union membership and its effect in the labour markets where the employer is a monopsony.** (15 marks)

■ ■ ■

Candidate's answer

(a) In the short term, there will be less time supplied owing to maximum working times. Supply shifts to the left, as shown in the diagram below.

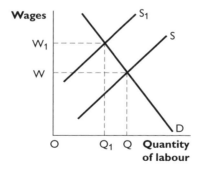

However, in the long run you would expect people to be happier at work — fewer days lost in stress-related illness, less absenteeism. Supply would then shift to the right.

Wages
For those paid on hourly rates, there may be a fall in take-home pay per worker in the short run, although hourly wages may rise. This is balanced by the argument that there is usually downward resistance in wages — workers will not accept lower take-home pay even if they are working for fewer hours. Firms may instead see profits squeezed or reduce employment levels as hourly wages rise even further.

d ata-response question 3

Employment levels
These may *fall* as the hourly cost per worker rises, or may increase, as more workers are required to cover the same output. We need to know the elasticity of demand and supply of labour that will determine the extent of wage rises.

12/15 marks

e This answer scores highly on evaluation because the short and the long term are strongly contrasted. The candidate shows what is likely to happen, then gives an alternative view. It is a pity that the *data* have not been used — these clearly outline the requested effects and the chance to earn up to 3 easy marks has been missed.

(b) Workers now have fairly powerful rights, as provided by the Social Chapter, signed in 1997, and other legislation such as the Equal Pay Act. Workers can now resort to the courts for many cases and do not need the unions, although of course trade unions often offer free or cheap legal aid. So it seems that many of the traditional roles of the unions are now no longer needed. The EU has provided rights for:
• parental leave
• consultation rights
• works councils
• equal rights for part-time and fixed-term workers
• maximum working time

However, unions are still powerful in some industries — the TUC figures show that utilities, the public sector and education are more than 50% unionised, with health and social work close to this at 46%. Trade unions still have impact in some sectors, for example the firefighters' dispute (2002–03). But the postal workers (September 2003) did not vote for strike action despite very low pay, because of fears of job losses in an ailing industry. As the General Secretary points out, it is a significant achievement that membership has stopped falling. **18/20 marks**

e This is a highly informed and well-balanced answer. This section would earn almost full marks because, although it may not be a perfect answer and bullet points should be avoided, the candidate demonstrates all of the skills required of an A2 student.

(c) *Income distribution*
It is possible that differentials will narrow, as there is more promotion to managerial positions, because people in high-up jobs will not be able to work for so long. This can be shown using the Lorenz curve, moving inwards towards the line of equality as the Gini coefficient decreases.

In the UK the distribution has become slightly more even since the introduction of the directive, but this may be for many other reasons, and as the directive has not yet fully come into force, it is not possible to say what has happened as a result.

Alternatively, those on the lowest incomes may be forced to cut back their hours, and many charities argue that in-work poverty is most damaging. If nurses had to restrict their hours, they might be unable to cover their costs of living.

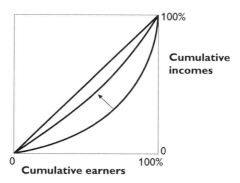

Flexibility

The UK labour market as a whole will become more rigid, but worker morale may improve. Firms might choose to relocate abroad — flexibility has been the UK's comparative advantage in recent years. **6/10 marks**

e The argument on income distribution shows some evaluation, but the flexibility argument does not answer the question directly.

(d) When a firm has monopsony power it can reduce wages in order to enjoy greater profits. The power of trade unions can act as a counterbalance to this labour market imperfection.

However, the increased rights of workers through legislation increase the relative power of the employee. In evaluation we should weigh up the decline in the unions as having both benefits and drawbacks, and offer an argument as to the future role of the unions. The Post Office dispute (September 2003) is a case where the employer is a monopsony. **7/15 marks**

e An answer such as this would be greatly helped by a diagram. While the candidate makes a decent attempt at application and evaluation, the analysis is very weak.

Scored 43/60 = grade A

Question 4

Redistribution

The chancellor's attempts to try to act like Robin Hood are not working.

Gordon Brown has been a highly redistributive chancellor. Income inequality has increased. Which statement is true? No need to ask the audience or to count the coughs: both are.

The Institute for Fiscal Studies (IFS) has totted up the effects of Mr Brown's six budgets since 1997. Its calculations showed that the chancellor has indeed been playing Robin Hood (see Figure 1). A lone parent, for example, is on average £24 a week better off in today's money as a result of Mr Brown — an 11% gain. Yet overall inequality has risen. A summary measure of the distribution of income is the 'Gini coefficient': the higher it is, in a range of 0 to 1, the more unequal income is. It has increased since Labour took office (see Figure 2).

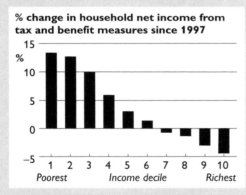

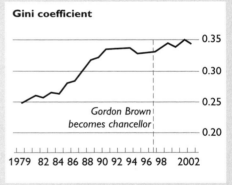

Figure 1 From rich to poor...   *Figure 2 ...but inequality still rises*

Mr Brown has been rowing against a powerful incoming tide. In order to isolate the effect of his measures, the IFS applied his schedules for taxes and benefits — which it assumed are fully claimed — to the latest estimate for underlying income. It then compared the net income of households with their position if Mr Brown had never been chancellor and if the taxes and benefits laid down in the last Conservative budget in 1996, uprated with inflation, were still in place.

The chancellor's problem is that the underlying income distribution has not remained frozen. Since 1996/97, for example, there has been a surge in the number of high-earners. According to the Inland Revenue, the number of people paying the top rate of income tax rose from 2.1 million in 1996/97 to 3.1 million in 2002/03. Furthermore, not everyone claims Mr Brown's new benefits, partly because his enthusiasm for means-testing makes them so complicated. The latest official estimates show that up to £4.5 billion worth of means-tested benefits are going unclaimed.

The chancellor prefers to avoid talking about egalitarianism directly, using phrases about reducing child and pensioner poverty. For example, the government has set a target to cut child poverty from 4.2 million in 1998/99 to 3.1 million in 2004/05. But this, too, is proving an uphill struggle. Figures released last month showed that there were still 3.8 million children in poverty in 2001/02, only 100,000 fewer than the year before.

Progress has been slow mainly because Mr Brown wants to cut relative, rather than absolute, poverty. His aim is to reduce the number of children living in households with incomes below 60% of median income (the level that divides the population, when ranked by income, into two). Households on median income will generally have at least one person in work, whereas many poor children live in households where no one works. So the government has been chasing a moving target as earnings have grown and more families have become two-earner households.

Mr Brown may find it easier to reduce inequality and to cut child poverty from now on. The troubles in the City and the bursting of the dotcom bubble mean there are fewer high-rollers than before. Employment is likely to stagnate rather than to rise as it did in the late 1990s.

But these are distinctly mixed blessings, since tax revenue will be less buoyant as a result. Whatever his aspirations to combat poverty, he would surely prefer to have the Treasury's coffers clinking rather than bare. Redistribution may sound like a lovely bit of fair-mindedness, but the only sure way to get there is through more poverty, not more wealth.

Source: 'Gordon Hood', *The Economist*, 5 April 2003.

(a) Assess the effectiveness of the government since 1997 in attempting to redistribute incomes. (15 marks)

(b) Discuss the effect of both the 'bursting of the dotcom bubble' and falling employment rates on income distribution. (20 marks)

(c) To what extent can the increase in inequality be explained by the government's changes in the tax and benefit system? (10 marks)

(d) Using the data from Figures 1 and 2, evaluate the impact on poverty that has resulted from recent policy changes. (15 marks)

■ ■ ■

Candidate's answer

(a) There has been economic growth in the UK since 1997 and so we would normally expect income differentials to widen. In the late 1980s boom, there was a great widening of income differentials. So, in a sense, the fact that differentials have not worsened is a sign of success. According to the article, you can only improve

data-response question 4

the living standards of the poor if you first make the rich better off through growth. This is just one opinion. You can have growth that is evenly distributed — it's just that it involves careful management and openness. And if you don't actively help the poor, they will suffer now — it's not just a case of 'a lovely bit of fair-minded-ness'. Yes, it may be that in the long run they may receive the benefits of growth, but as Keynes said, 'in the long run we are all dead'. **11/15 marks**

e There is a lot in the article that has not been used. Using the passage not only offers easy marks, but also helps to keep you focused on the wording of the question. It is good to see some critical distance — where the passage is used, the answer picks up on bias in the article. However, try to avoid sounding political in your answers — there is an important difference between being opinionated and having justified opinions.

(b) In a recession, income differentials become narrower. In the UK the dotcom bursting has not caused a recession yet, but the article suggests that unemployment will rise. If unemployment rises, you would expect differentials to widen — those out of work will be a lot worse off than the average income earners. **7/20 marks**

e The analysis starts well, but there are likely to be 8 marks available for evaluation on this question. A common error is made, too: the question refers to *employment*, not *unemployment*.

(c) Inequality has been rising, but at a slower rate. Changes in the tax and benefit system have not been sufficient to reverse the tide, but they have had *some* impact on redistribution Robin-Hood style: means-tested benefits have increased, and there have been cuts in income tax in the lower tax bands. There have been real increases in child benefit, and as these affect everyone with children, the proportionate effect on poorer families is likely to be greater. **5/10 marks**

e The logic of this answer is perfectly acceptable. There is reference to the data, but there are gaps in the analysis, and there is no evaluation.

(d) The tax and benefit system changes have been redistributive — taking from the rich and giving to the poor. However, this effect has not outweighed the increasing inequality as shown by the increasing Gini coefficient. The higher the figure, the more unequal is the income distribution. **9/15 marks**

e Again, there is little evaluation; for this reason alone the grade would not be above C. In addition, the question focuses on *poverty* rather than inequality.

Scored 32/60 = grade C

Question 5

Pensioner poverty under Labour

Since coming to power in 1997, the Labour government has introduced significant and historically large increases in means-tested benefits for pensioners in the form of the minimum income guarantee (MIG). The MIG is a means-tested benefit that replaced income support for those aged 60 and above. It supplements the incomes of the poorest people in this age bracket to ensure that they receive a set minimum level of income. The basic value of the MIG (in April 2003) for eligible single people was £102.10 and for couples it was £155.80. These rates correspond to real increases in excess of 30% since 1997.

These reforms were designed to raise pensioner living standards considerably, especially among the poorest. In official government statistics, the government uses a 'headcount ratio' to track poverty. Under a headcount ratio approach, an individual is defined as living in poverty if his or her household income, once adjusted for household size and composition, falls below some poverty line. The headcount ratio is then simply defined as the proportion of individuals living in poverty.

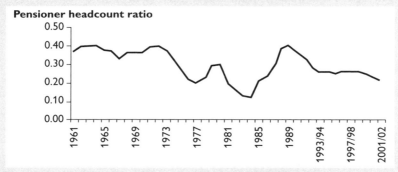

Source: *Family Expenditure Survey* and *Family Resources Survey*.

Figure 1 Pensioner poverty, 1961–2001/02

Tracking the headcount ratio over time, we are able to trace the evolution of pensioner poverty. This is shown in Figure 1, where the before-mentioned relative poverty line is used. There are two main features to be taken from this figure. First, there has been a large reduction in poverty over time. In the early 1960s around 40% of pensioners were in poverty on this measure. This contrasts with today, when only just over 20% of pensioners are in poverty. This is a general reflection of pensioners becoming better off, both in real terms and relative to the population as a whole. However, perhaps more notable than this is the fact that the series is highly volatile over time. Indeed, over the 5-year period from 1984 to 1989 pensioner poverty actually tripled.

data-response question 5

> From Figure 1 we see that pensioner poverty has been remarkably stable throughout the 1990s. Much of this period has been one of consistently high economic growth, with median incomes increasing by an average of around 3% per annum under Labour. Other things being equal, we would expect this to increase pensioner poverty, so standing still is itself an achievement.
>
> But given the large recent increases in means-tested benefits, we may have expected pensioner poverty to fall further than it actually has. One possible explanation for this is the non-take-up of state benefits. Indeed official statistics suggest that between 22% and 36% of pensioners who are entitled to MIG do not claim it. A similar proportion of pensioners do not claim council tax benefit and about one in ten do not claim their housing benefit entitlement. Full take-up of these benefits would reduce measured pensioner poverty by 1.7%.
>
> Source: A. Shepherd, 'Pensioner poverty under Labour', *Economic Review*, vol. 21, no. 1, September 2003.

(a) **Assess the argument for linking pensions to average earnings rather than the rate of inflation.** (15 marks)

(b) **Evaluate means testing as a method of topping up pension deficiencies.** (15 marks)

(c) **'Over the 5-year period from 1984 to 1989 pensioner poverty actually tripled.' Assess two factors that might explain such a phenomenon.** (20 marks)

(d) **Discuss the problems involved in using a headcount measure of poverty.** (10 marks)

■ ■ ■

Candidate's answer

(a) Linking pensions to average earnings would mean that pensioners would not move into relative poverty when incomes rise faster than inflation. One famous example was the 75p pensions increase based on the RPI in September 2000 when average incomes were rising much more quickly. This widens the inequality, because pensions are usually well below average income. Relative poverty increases. The problem with linking pensions to average incomes is the COST. **12/15 marks**

> *e* The argument is well presented, with useful examples and evaluation. You don't, however, need to use CAPITALS — examiners don't need to be shouted at, and they prefer power in your reasoning rather than in your tone of voice!

(b) One of the main problems of means testing is non-take-up of benefits. This might look like the government is saving money, but in practice it may mean that some people live in extreme poverty and cannot look after themselves properly, and this might actually cost the government more. For example, many pensioners do not claim their heating allowance, and cannot afford to heat their houses properly in the winter. Other reasons why there is low take-up may be the hassle of claiming, information costs and the stigma of claiming.

However, on the other side of the argument, those who have the least to gain are less likely to claim. Those who don't feel poor or indeed are not prepared to state their money situation may not realise that they can claim, and it's a waste of money to give these people benefits. **14/15 marks**

e There is a good attempt here at evaluation — the candidate sees both sides of means testing. However, evaluation doesn't mean being patronising. Avoid getting political or moralistic.

(c) The pensioner poverty rate changes in line with the economic cycle. In other words, pensioner poverty tends to increase in times of high economic growth, and decrease when growth is low. On a measure like this it would appear that the best way of reducing pensioner poverty would be to trigger a severe recession. There are two main reasons for this trend. The first is that pensioner incomes tend to be quite stable over the economic cycle, with pensions often only linked to prices, if at all. This means that pensioners tend to fall behind non-pensioners in relative terms at times of high earnings growth. The size of these changes can also be explained by the pensioner income distribution being quite narrowly spread, so that even small changes in the poverty line can shift many pensioners either side of it. **12/20 marks**

e This is an informed answer, but the argument needs much clearer signposts. It is not clear when the first reason stops and the second begins. It is wise to spell them out separately — and don't be afraid to leave a few lines between the two in case you think of more to say on the first point. It's amazing how many marks are awarded to scrunched up 'last thoughts' in the margin — better to spread your answer out from the start.

(d) The headcount measure gives the proportion of people living in relative poverty. There are two main problems: one is, at what level is relative poverty really a problem in the West, and two, how far below the poverty line does the distribution spread, since the poverty rate is the same whether individuals are just below or far below the poverty line? In the UK the poverty line is said to be 60% of median income, but this is not related to need or hardships. Median incomes have grown by almost 10% in real terms between 2000 and 2002, which means the poverty line will also have been increasing — more people will have been falling into poverty in other words, if there have been smaller changes to pensions, even though their income has actually been rising. The headcount measure is therefore a sliding target. If we used an absolute poverty line, which increases with prices rather than incomes, then a much more notable reduction in pensioner poverty would have been achieved since 1997. **6/10 marks**

e Two valid problems are raised, and there is application to facts about the UK as well as some convincing analysis. However, this answer illustrates a common failing — only one point is fully developed.

Scored 44/60 = grade A

Question 6

The labour market under New Labour

Between 1960 and 1979 living standards in the UK rose faster than in earlier periods but less than in most other OECD countries. By 1979, GDP per head had fallen well below that of Canada, Germany, Sweden and France. Italy and Japan caught up with the UK on this measure of wealth. After 1979 the UK's relative performance improved. Since 1997, under Labour, the UK has maintained its strong growth relative to other countries.

Table 1 *Annual growth rates of GDP, population, employment, inflation, productivity and hours worked over two administrations*

	Conservative 1979–96	Labour 1997–2002
GDP (% change)	2.2	2.6
Working age population (% change)	0.5	0.6
Employment (% change)	0.3	1.1
Unemployment rate (% points)	0.1	−0.5
Inactivity rate (% points)	0.03	−0.03
GDP per employee (%)	1.9	1.5
Average weekly hours worked (%)	−0.2	−0.5
GDP per hour worked	2.1	1.9
Inflation (% points)	6.5	2.4

As Table 1 shows, growth during the years of the Labour administration has been somewhat faster than during the longer Conservative era. Under Labour, growth has been extremely jobs rich. This means that productivity growth, as measured by output per worker, has been weaker than in the Conservative years. Historically, as living standards rose, individuals and institutions settled on shorter working hours, which allowed more time to enjoy increased wealth. Unusually this trend stopped during the Conservative era. Despite there being more part-time work, this was largely offset by longer hours among the professional and managerial classes. As documented by Green, average hours of work have fallen sharply since the mid-1990s. This is in part due to increased holiday entitlements resulting from the implementation of the European Working Time Directive, but also because of a reduction in the numbers of managerial staff working very long hours. Hence, productivity growth adjusted for hours of work is quite similar over the two administrations.

When Labour took office, it announced its intention of following international guidelines by giving greater prominence to the International Labour Office (ILO) definition of unemployment, rather than the claimant count based on the numbers eligible to receive benefit, which was, and remains, susceptible to changes in eligibility rules. (Despite this the government was rather quick to take credit when the claimant count fell back below 1 million in 2001!) Both counts were falling before 1997 but continued to fall thereafter. The ILO unemployment rate has now hovered around 5% — some 1.5 million individuals — for the last 2 years. This is around half the level observed in 1993 and about 30% below the level inherited in 1997. As a result, some commentators have concluded, perhaps rather rashly, that the labour market is now close to full employment. Still, there is little sign of substantial inflationary pressure stemming from the labour market. This has led some to revise down, again, their estimates of the NAIRU (the rate of unemployment below which inflationary pressure starts to build). Any worries that the labour market could sustain a 5% unemployment rate without degenerating due to substantial inflationary pressures caused by labour shortages have proved unfounded. Notice that the massive pay rises awarded recently to chief executives and footballers will not in themselves generate higher inflation because the number of individuals affected is small. The justification, behaviour and impression associated with these awards are, of course, very different matters.

Long-term unemployment, aside from the human cost, is thought of as a significant indicator of wage pressure. Long-term unemployment has also continued to fall to low levels, partly due to the New Deal policies introduced by Labour aimed at helping the long-term unemployed back to work raising employment by about 17,000 a year.

However, labour market performance should not be assessed solely on the basis of the unemployment numbers. Unemployment can fall because individuals leave the labour force rather than find a job. It is therefore just as important to monitor what is happening to employment.

EU members have recently agreed on the European Employment Strategy. This is essentially a set of targets aimed at promoting full employment and social cohesion in member countries. The targets were based on employment, rather than unemployment, rates, with an aspiration that each country should have an aggregate employment rate of 70% by 2010, a 60% employment rate among women and a 50% employment rate among those aged 55 and over.

ata-response question 6

As Table 2 shows, Britain had already reached these objectives in 1990.

Table 2 Britain's employment performance, 1975–2002

	Total		Men		Women		All 55+		Lone parents
	000s	%	000s	%	000s	%	000s	%	%
1975	22,560	72.7	14,180	87.8	8,380	56.4	3,100	72.5	n/a
1979	23,400	73.3	14,410	86.8	8,990	58.6	3,200	69.2	51.5
1984	22,370	67.4	13,330	76.6	9,030	57.3	2,590	57.5	41.3
1990	25,560	75.0	14,690	82.4	10,870	66.8	2,470	58.8	44.0
1993	24,030	70.1	13,410	74.8	10,620	64.9	2,260	54.0	42.1
1997	25,140	72.5	14,060	77.4	11,080	67.0	2,340	55.6	45.3
2000	26,220	74.3	14,650	79.2	11,570	68.9	2,610	58.4	49.9
2002	26,760	74.4	14,900	79.0	11,860	69.4	2,940	60.6	53.2

Note: population of working age (men 16–64, women 16–59). Figures weighted and rounded to the nearest 10,000. 55+ columns are men and women added together.

Source: R. Dickens, P. Gregg and J. Wadsworth, 'The labour market under New Labour', *Economic Review*, vol. 21, no. 1, September 2003.

(a) Discuss two possible causes of the changes in employment levels indicated in Table 1. (15 marks)

(b) To what extent has the New Deal 'helped the long-term unemployed back to work'? (20 marks)

(c) Using the data, examine the changing structure of employment in the UK. (15 marks)

(d) What factors might explain the 'jobs-rich' UK growth? (10 marks)

■ ■ ■

Candidate's answer

(a) The aggregate employment rate has fallen and risen with the subsequent economic cycle, but these overall employment rates are increasing. So in part this is due to strong GDP growth, but also rises in productivity, low inflation and low unemployment — i.e. we're more efficient.

There has been a net gain of 2.5 million jobs since 1993 and 1.5 million since 1997. The improvement among lone parents has been dramatic. Many of these will be part time. It is largely a result of the WFTC. **9/15 marks**

This is an accurate account, but it contains no evaluation, so the mark is capped at 9/15.

(b) The long-term unemployed find it harder to get jobs and so do not constitute part of the reserve army of labour, which keeps wages down. The New Deal offers training to help people get jobs — the deal is that they must accept jobs that are offered, and the Job-Seeker's Allowance will be paid for a maximum of 6 months. One important point is that the New Deal only applies to young workers. To some extent this does help long-term unemployed back to work, but evidence suggests that many will work for a week or so and then start the whole process again. However, even if this is the case, at least the long-term unemployed have a strong incentive to go to work, have training to help them achieve this, and do some work! There are enormous external benefits such as improved morale, reduced crime, and the opportunity for some to get out of the unemployment trap.

14/20 marks

> 🖉 This is well informed and addresses both sides of the argument. However, it is too brief for a 20-mark question — remember that about four factors should be given for these questions.

(c) Employment is rising in absolute terms, fairly steadily from 1975 at 22.5 million to 26.8 million now. This is 74.4% of the working population, which means that 25% of people of working age are economically inactive. Activity rates have also been rising since 1975.

Male employment has not changed much, but male participation rates have fallen. This must mean that men are leaving the labour force, while the number of those of working age has risen. Female employment has risen by a third over the period shown, and activity rates have risen.

The trend has been for fewer workers to work past the age of 55, but that has recently been reversed. This is probably owing to the pension crisis — people need to work longer to get enough to maintain their living standards.

More lone parents are returning to work. This may be because of improved child-care arrangements in the UK, but it may be a sign that the WFTC and child tax credit are having an effect. Both are paid relative to income.   **9/15 marks**

> 🖉 It is a clumsy use of the data to say that activity rates have risen — there were substantial falls within the period after the recessions of the early 1980s and 1990s. Some reasons for this could have been suggested. The data are used comprehensively, but *critical* use of data would add evaluative marks. Notice that the choice of years is not even, and no allowance is made for changes in the economic cycle. Population statistics would help in the analysis — how else can we fully explain rising employment alongside falling participation rates?

(d) Jobs-rich growth has occurred because more people are working or working longer hours. This raises GDP, but it is not necessarily good for standards of living. It is good to have jobs-rich growth if there is a vast pool of unemployed resources, but if the labour market is tight then there is likely to be upward pressure on wages.

d ata-response question 6

The opposite of jobs-rich growth might be productivity growth, which means people can work less and yet still GDP rises. Factors that might explain growth without rising productivity might be:

- union power — maintain workforce levels, in line with productivity
- minimum working time directive — you cannot grow by making people work longer — you have to employ more people
- growth of the tertiary, service sector. You cannot economise on workers in the service industry — indeed, in times of improving standards of living, people expect increasing service standards. **5/10 marks**

e This is a classic case of raising too many points but not going deep enough. The answer also begins with an introduction that does not actually address the question. The content that would earn the marks is bullet pointed, which is often a danger sign — no real analysis can be done in such short paragraphs, let alone evaluation. Use bullet points to *learn*, but not to build up evaluative responses.

Scored 37/60 = grade B